INTUITIVE EATING

A Non-Diet Workbook To Find The Satisfaction-Factor, Overcome Deprivation And Guilt And Stop Emotional And Binge Eating

BY
ALISSON POT.

© Copyright 2019 by Alisson Pot All rights reserved.

This document is geared towards providing exact and reliable information with regards to the topic and issue covered. The publication is sold with the idea that the publisher is not required to render accounting, officially permitted, or otherwise, qualified services. If advice is necessary, legal or professional, a practiced individual in the profession should be ordered.

From a Declaration of Principles which was accepted and approved equally by a Committee of the American Bar Association and a Committee of Publishers and Associations.

In no way is it legal to reproduce, duplicate, or transmit any part of this document in either electronic means or in printed format. Recording of this publication is strictly prohibited and any storage of this document is not allowed unless with written permission from the publisher. All rights reserved

The information provided herein is stated to be truthful and consistent, in that any liability, in terms of inattention or otherwise, by any usage or abuse of any policies, processes, or directions contained within is the solitary and utter responsibility of the recipient reader. Under no circumstances will any legal responsibility or blame be held against the publisher for any reparation, damages, or monetary loss due to the information herein, either directly or indirectly.

Respective authors own all copyrights not held by the publisher.

The information herein is offered for informational purposes solely, and is universal as so. The presentation of the information is without contract or any type of guarantee assurance.

The trademarks that are used are without any consent, and the publication of the trademark is without permission or backing by the trademark owner. All trademarks and brands within this book are for clarifying purposes only and are the owned by the owners themselves, not affiliated with this document.

WHY YOU SHOULD READ THIS BOOK

I know, you probably think that you have to be on a diet forever to lose weight permanently. But nothing could be further from the truth. With rare exceptions, most people were born. But nothing could be further from the truth. With rare exceptions, most people were born in normal-weight bodies. But then we learned to nourish instead of eating intuitively.

Dieting puts the body in survival mode. A diet itself triggers the intense biological urge to ingest large amounts of high-calorie foods. It causes the instinctive instincts of the body to override all intellectual controls. It prepares the body to maximize food intake and minimize energy consumption.

Diets have led us to fight against our own bodily survival, the body's most basic instinct.

Imagine how difficult life would be if you had to go to the toilet on a fixed schedule. What if you only watered three times a day?

At 20.00, 12.00 and 18.00 you could release exactly 5 ounces. Of course they would measure it to make sure it was the right amount. If you need more, you have to wait until the next scheduled time. And too bad, if you had to leave at 10 in the morning, hold it until noon.

You would be unhappy. Your body would have a hard time keeping to an arbitrary schedule. It would probably be ugly.

Excessive eating, because your body refuses to starve, does not make you a failure. It means that you are human.

* It does not make you sick.

* It does not mean that you are forever flawed.

* It does not make you sick and tries to make you feel better for the rest of your life.

* It means that at the time you did the best you could.

* It means that you can forgive yourself and keep going.

Intuitive eating is the most natural thing we do, and your body knows exactly what it takes to live at its best. You just have to practice listening and accessing the information. Your body knows what to do. Just as it can breathe, reproduce and heal.

Remember how children live, we can learn a lot from them ...

* They rest when they are tired.

* They run, jump, swim, dance and play as much as they can because it feels good and fun.

* They are picky about what they eat. They will starve rather than settle for something they do not love.

* They eat when they are hungry.

* If they feel full, they must be tricked or bribed to eat another bite.

* They drink when they are thirsty.

* They love their bodies and do not care what their thighs look like or whether their tummy is not flat and tight.

* You do not have to think about it all. It comes naturally and easily as part of being human.

All these natural instincts live in each one of us.

We all have the innate ability to take care of ourselves. We just have to remember. We just have to get used to listening to our bodies ... following their wisdom. Remember, normal body weight is your birthright. It was stolen from you. Now, with intuitive food, you can take it back.

So stop being fat forever. They are not condemned to being overweight or constantly feeding. Let overeating and obesity disappear in the past. They have served you well to keep you alive. Once you stop nourishing and accepting the body that you were born with, you can return to your unique, normal weight.

I do not suggest that every model will be skinny. The endless tyrannical pressure to be very thin is a big part of the problem. Some bodies should be soft and curvy. Others are sharp and angular by nature. We are different stocky, tall, fleshy, muscular, sinewy, short, etc. The variety is wonderfully beautiful.

Accepting and loving the unique beauty of your body will heal and free you. Be like a child and enjoy the body that you have. Appreciate the power in your muscles. Enjoy the feeling of being alive on this planet. Let go, to look in a certain direction. Be yourself. Let someone try to be like the models or celebrities. The world will be a better place to have the real, unique, special person that YOU are.

Believe in your own healing. Believe that you can live easily and naturally with your own ideal weight.

This belief is a big part of what will set you free. Intuitive food is normal and completely natural. Deep inside, you know how to do it.

Table of Contents

Introduction 1

Chapter 1: Eating Disorders 8

Chapter 2: How To Stop Binge Eating And Get Back In The Driver's Seat 20

Chapter 3: Conscious Eating For The Holidays 25

Chapter 4: Mindful And Gentle Eating Process - How To Interrupt The Pattern Of Emotional Eating 32

Top 10 Tips For Eating Disorder Recovery - Self Acceptance, Health & Well Being 39

Chapter 5: Mindful And Gentle Eating - The Value Of Slowing Down And Tasting Your Food 45

Chapter 6: The Secret To Ending Emotional Eating 54

Chapter 7: Eating Rules To Follow To Lose Weight And Body Fat 62

Chapter 8: Don't Stop Eating Fat To Lose Weight .. 65

Chapter 9: How To Lose Weight By Eating For Energy 68

Chapter 10: Calorie Reality---Eating Healthier But Still Gaining Weight 72

Chapter 11: Do Units Acquire Intuition? 117

Chapter 12: Using Your Intuition To Make Decisions To Save Time 126

Chapter 13: Reasons Why Listening To Your Intuition Is Important! 128

Chapter 14: Ways Your Intuition Talks To You 132

Chapter 15: Eating Disorders - Coaching Yourself To Recovery 136

Chapter 16: Trusting Your Intuition - You Already Know What To Do 146

Chapter 17: Relationships: Why Do Some Women Ignore Their Intuition? 153

Chapter 18: Big Mistakes That Block Your Intuition 160

Chapter 19: Intuitive Leadership - Listening To Your Intuition 168

Chapter 20: Core Beliefs That Hinders Overcoming Challenges 175

Chapter 21: How To Overcome Self-Sabotage And Move Forward 183

Chapter 22: Understanding, Developing And Using Our Intuition 191

Chapter 23: Sleep Deprivation - The Facts 201

References 204

INTRODUCTION

Most people are nutritionally unbalanced. The imbalance seems to be due to a lack of vitamins and minerals in the diet. The vitamins most likely to be out of balance are vitamin D3, vitamin B12 and folic acid. Other vitamins may be missing, but most people are missing them. In addition to vitamins, most people have a lack of trace elements and some a lack of potassium and magnesium.

By alleviating these shortcomings that seem to alleviate most of the symptoms of overeating, people seem to be more in tune with themselves, and their eating habits can become more intuitive. When you drink more water, you realize that you are not so hungry, so you first drink water when you notice hunger signals. You begin to interpret better when you are hungry and when you are full. You can better decide what and how much you want to eat.

Intuitive Eating

With intuitive eating, people are not so worried about their body shape or how others see them. By focusing on how their body feels, they are better able to make smart food choices and improve their portion control. Their body size and shape naturally adapts to their ideal size.

People who adjust to their bodies have a much greater sense of self-esteem, a higher stress response threshold, to make them calmer, more optimistic, happier and more positive. They do not count calories or fat grams, do not drink disgusting diet drinks, and do not go hungry.

To start your process more intuitively in your eating style, you must discard all your diet books. You have rules that are imposed on you that will throw you into radio and make you feel guilty that another diet has failed. Stop the yo-yo effect. Diets work only when you're there, and most of them are unsustainable as part of a lifestyle choice.

If you think you are hungry, drink two glasses of water and wait a few minutes. If you are still hungry, for goodness sakes eat something. If you wait until you are over hungry, the food stuffing monster will appear and you will be out of control. It is actually best to eat five or six small meals or snacks in a day than to wait until you are over hungry.

Plan your mini-meals, so you know what you are going to be eating and you have all those good nutritious foods in the house. Intuit what your body would like to eat and incorporate as many colors and textures in your meals and snacks as possible. If you can do some raw, all the better. If your body needs something sweet, try making hot chocolate with almond milk and cocoa, sweetened with Stevia.

Intuitive Eating

Let go of all your negative judgments around food. All of the things you should eat and all of the things you shouldn't are all surrounded by judgments lodged in your emotions. By creating a clear space around your food and your eating habits you become more intuitive as you develop your clarity.

Eat slowly and observe your body's signals. How does your food taste? Are you comfortably full yet? Don't be afraid to cover your food and refrigerate it until the next time you eat. It is not necessary to eat all the food on your plate. If you notice you are still hungry, by all means eat something else.

Be satisfied. The pleasure of eating delicious food in comfortable surroundings goes a long way to satisfy our hunger and our emotions around food. By eating in this way, you discover it takes much less food to bring you to a place of satisfaction.

Alisson Pot

If you're bummed out, recognize and deal with your emotions without eating. Notice that you are feeling down and recognize you are not in danger of exploding or other imminent disaster. You are feeling down at the moment but you will feel better. Food is to nourish your body, not to stuff into yourself for comfort. Do what you can to change the habit of using food for comfort.

Change the rules around food. Recognize when you are hungry and eat then. Do not eat when you are not. Any other excuse to eat is just that, an excuse. Have some character and some discipline around food. If you crave a carton of Chocolate Brownie Overload Ice Cream, make yourself a cup of hot chocolate with almond milk and Stevia. Make an agreement with yourself to break your food addictions. You will feel better for it and you can be more in control of what goes into your mouth.

Intuitive Eating

No matter what you think you look like, respect yourself and love yourself no matter what your judgments are. The most critical eye in the world is yours. No one can be more self-critical than you and pick you apart like you can. Change your habit of your constant critiquing and let yourself be who you really are. If all your relatives are round, you may have to be satisfied that you are round. You are not a horrible person if you have a muffin waist or a double chin.

Put on some walking shoes and go for a walk. If all you can manage right now is going to the end of the block and back then you have done the best you can. Celebrate your achievements and look forward to walking around the block. By being in tune with yourself, you can progress at your own pace. Noticing how you feel and what progress you are making is a positive step.

Alisson Pot

Know that you are the only person that can restore your health and your waistline by making healthier food choices. Choose tasty, nutritious food that you feel good eating. Know that as you eat better you will feel better. As you feel better, you will want to feel even better. You will be encouraged by your progress and you will let your intuition guide you as you walk this new road of empowerment.

CHAPTER 1

Eating Disorders

Research reports that two out of four young people have unhealthy ideas about eating, dieting and weight. With the alarming increase of eating disorders, dieting, and obesity among children as young as 5 and 6, it's crucial these days for parents to proactively work to promote healthy eating and body image in their children.

It has been found that in households where mom talks about feeling fat, 81% of their teenage daughters said they felt fat too. Our girls, especially, are being easily confused and influenced when it comes to body image development. In a culture where young people are bombarded with skinny, glossy, and superficial images, parents can be a mirror reflecting understanding, reassurance, wisdom, and love that their children can look into with faith and not fear.

Many factors influence whether an adolescent will develop a positive or negative body image. As a parent, you can learn to be supportive the next time your child says, "Mom, I feel fat or Mom, I hate my life," and be ready with an answer by saying, "that sounds like an important feeling, tell me more."

The Slenderizing Beauty Ideal

Everyday 56% of the women in the United States are on diets. We have a 30-billion-dollar-a-year diet industry. The historical view of the ideal female body has changed over the years and influenced this dieting America. Although many factors contribute to the changing body shape of girls, including better nutrition, earlier onset of puberty and other societal influences. The fact remains that regardless of the reason, the common trend over time points to a slenderizing standard of the female ideal.

With standards like this, it is no wonder that children are dissatisfied with their bodies.

When it came to looks – teens are most concerned about weight. A Teen People survey of 1000 teens, showed that 39% worried about weight. Between 2000 and 2001, cosmetic surgery on girls 18 and younger had increased by 22%.

Another study reported that after girls viewed pictures of models in fashion magazines:

- 69% reported that magazine pictures influenced their idea of the perfect body shape and
- 47% reported wanting to lose weight because of magazine pictures.

This study found that those who were frequent readers of fashion magazines were 2-3 times more likely than infrequent readers to start dieting to lose weight because of a magazine article.

What Are Eating Disorders?

Is it any wonder, then, that eating disorders affect 7 million women and 1 million men in the United States? Eating disorders include anorexia, bulimia nervosa and binge-eating disorder. People with anorexia starve themselves to dangerously thin levels, at least 15% below their appropriate weight. People with bulimia binge uncontrollably on large amounts of food--sometimes thousands of calories at a time--and then purge the calories out of their bodies through vomiting, starving, excessive exercise, laxatives, or other methods. People with binge-eating disorder eat uncontrollably, but they do not purge the calories.

Intuitive Eating

Eating Disorders Not Otherwise Specified (or EDNOS) is a new classification of disordered eating that falls between anorexia, binge eating and bulimia. Unfortunately, since this type of 'sub-clinical' disorder is often not life-threatening, there appears to be little research available on the topic. One of the goals at FINDINGbalance.com, the first national organization dedicated to helping those who struggle with ENDOS, is to begin collecting new information through input from their website visitors and other existing sources.

Anorexia Warning Signs for Adolescents & Adults:

- Loss of menstrual period
- Dieting obsessively when not overweight
- Claiming to feel "fat" when overweight is not a reality
- Preoccupation with food, calories, nutrition, and/or cooking

- Denial of hunger
- Excessive exercising, being overly active
- Frequent weighing
- Strange food-related behaviors
- Episodes of binge-eating
- 15% or more below normal body weight/rapid weight loss
- Depression
- Slowness of thought/memory difficulties
- Hair loss

* In children any combination of these symptoms should be considered serious and an immediate evaluation by an eating disorder professional or physician is recommended.

Bulimia Warning Signs:

- Excessive concern about weight

Intuitive Eating

- Strict dieting followed by eating binges
- Frequent overeating, especially when distressed.
- Bingeing on high calorie, sweet foods
- Use of laxatives, diuretics, strict dieting, vigorous exercise, and/or vomiting to control weight
- Leaving for the bathroom after meals
- Being secretive about binges or vomiting
- Planning binges or opportunities to binge
- Feeling out of control
- Depressive moods

EDNOS Warning Signs:

- You're always on a diet, always coming off a diet, or always getting ready to go on one again (chronic dieting).

- You categorize foods as 'safe' and 'off limits', but weigh within normal ranges and are not participating in bulimia.

- You eliminate entire food groups from your diet.

- You are obsessed with exercising but eat fairly regularly.

- You binge and/or purge occasionally, but not more than a few times a month.

- You skip social occasions because you feel fat, or because you are afraid of what's being served, yet your weight is normal.

- You believe that everyone is as focused on your weight as you are.

- You refuse to eat regular meals, choosing instead to 'nibble' throughout the day on small portions of food (which usually leads to bingeing).

How Common Are Eating Disorders?

Intuitive Eating

Eating disorders are serious illnesses. The malnourishment of both anorexia and bulimia affects the body rapidly and can lead to hypoglycemia, pancreatitis, enlargement of the heart, heart attacks, congestive heart failure, permanent brain shrinkage with loss of memory and IQ, infertility, and osteoporosis. It is not uncommon for a teenage girl with anorexia to have the bones of an 80 year old woman. The condition is not reversible. Ultimately, approximately, 6% of people with anorexia and 1% with bulimia will die from their eating disorder.

According to Remuda Ranch, an inpatient eating disorder treatment center in Arizona, estimates indicate that 1/3 of American women and 15% of men will have an eating disorder or related problem at some time in their lives. Fifty years ago, eating disorders were practically unheard of. Research suggest a strong genetic component to eating disorders. People who are prone to perfectionism and low self-esteem may be most at risk.

In today's world, the cultural pressures for young people to obtain and maintain super-thin bodies are extreme. In this environment, thinness readily becomes a way of dealing with many emotional issues. However, outcome studies have shown there is much hope for people with eating disorders. The good news is that approximately 75% of patients with eating disorders do recover.

How Can Parents Prevent Disordered Eating?

Parents can do much to spare their children a life-long struggle with eating and weight. One of the most important ways is to examine their own beliefs and prejudices as a parent about weight and appearance. Parents should communicate acceptance and respect for themselves and other people regardless of weight.

This will reduce some of the pressure children may feel to change their bodies. Especially, discourage the idea that a particular diet or body size can reliably lead to happiness. Do not model or encourage dieting. Accept and talk about the fact that diets don't work and the dangers of altering one's body through dieting.

Tips For Healthy Eating

In our diet crazed culture, what really is healthy eating? Here are a few tips that will go a long way in feeding your family a balanced mealtime experience. For starters, teach your children to listen to their body -- eat when you're hungry, stop when you're full. Remember balance means that most of the time you eat because you are hungry and use food as fuel for your body. But, it also means that sometimes you eat simply when the food appeals to you or when it is appropriate in a social setting (e.g., popcorn at the movies), allowing yourself to eat for enjoyment.

Try to eat different foods everyday, in other words, create an adventure for your taste buds. Aim to inspire your family to eat 3 meals and 1 to 3 snacks a day. The idea that snacking between meals is bad is a thing of the past. By teaching your kids to eat every 2 to 4 hours, they will prevent their body from getting overly hungry which could set them up to overeat later. Plus, the body uses the fuel from food very efficiently when smaller amounts of food is eaten more frequently throughout the day.

The bottom line: eat normally, exercise moderately, and let your body weigh what it wants. Yes, it will take courage and perseverance, but the rewards of knowing you are teaching your family how to eat for pleasure is a true legacy to leave.

CHAPTER 2

How To Stop Binge Eating And Get Back In The Driver's Seat

Binge eating is eating "gone wrong." Binge eating is eating gone on automatic pilot, eating disconnected from physical body sensations like fullness and hunger. After a binge you may experience a glazed feeling and a "coming back to awareness." "What happened here?" and "I wish I could undo that" are common thoughts.

Mindful eating is the opposite of bingeing. Mindful eating, conscious eating, and intuitive eating are all terms to describe eating that occurs when the mind and the body are in full communication.

When this process is happening, we eat in response to our body cues and our body's needs. We eat what we are hungry for and we eat until we are full (not stuffed). We are conscious of how we are feeling while we are eating and how we are likely to feel afterwards. Conscious eating does not leave us stuffed to the gills, sick to our stomachs and collapsed on the couch, too uncomfortable to move.

Conscious eating fuels us and gives us energy. The food we eat consciously gives our bodies and our minds pleasure. It is a nice experience.

To stop binge eating, the first requirement is to turn off the automatic pilot and get back into the driver's seat. This takes practice and won't be easy the first or second time you try it. Like using a muscle though, your ability to stop a binge will grow stronger.

Try these tips:

Slow down. Don't try to stop the binge at first, but communicate to yourself what you are doing. This means you are not on auto-pilot. Say to yourself out loud or in your head "I feel a binge coming on" or "Here we go" or "I'm starting to feel out of control with my eating." Make the process conscious.

Put your food on a plate. You've heard this before because it's important. To be mindfully eating you need to be experiencing the food and how much of it you are choosing to eat.

Practice being a nonjudgmental observer. Try to notice what both your head and your body are doing--from a curious nonjudgmental standpoint.

What's the dialogue going on in your brain? Is it silent, are you numb, are you criticizing yourself or already planning how you'll do it differently tomorrow? Don't try to change your thoughts, just be curious and collect data about what your mind is doing. Now put your hand on your stomach. Take a deep breath. Try to pay attention to how your body is feeling. Feel your hand on your stomach. Feel it move as you breath. Try to take note--nonjudgmentally of how your body feels. Is there tension anywhere, muscle tightness, are you holding your breath or breathing deeply? Does your stomach feel full or empty? How full? How empty?

If you feel courageous, put your other hand on your heart. Feel your heart beat. Keep breathing. Ask yourself what you are REALLY hungry for. Ask yourself what you could feed your self and your spirit IN ADDITION TO food. Sit for a minute and listen. Don't worry or be afraid if you don't know the answer this time. It's asking the question that is important.

Afterwards, if you can do it, try to write down what you noticed about the whole experience. Work very hard not to be critical but to write from the standpoint of a curious observer. As you think about what happened, can you identify anything that brought you to that binge? What was going on before? When did you decide to do it? Can you identify how you were feeling--both in your mind (bored, lonely, happy, sad) and in your body (tired, tense, hungry)?

Practice doing one small, nice, compassionate thing for your body and soul every day that has nothing to do with food. It doesn't have to be earth shattering. Put your feet up and sit for fifteen minutes before you tackle the laundry, take a bubble bath instead of a shower, wear something that you feel lovely in, put music on that you love, kick off your shoes and wiggle your toes.

CHAPTER 3

Conscious Eating For The Holidays

Are you already counting the pounds you will gain this holiday season? Many people feel obligated to prepare and eat traditional foods during the holidays in order to please Mom, Grandma and very heritage they were born into! It's just the right thing to do-isn't it? Our weight-obsessed society pulls out the stops and eats cookies, cakes, pies and breads in quantities they would never consider throughout the rest of the year. In fact, good manners dictate that you not only eat these foods, but gift them to others as well, and this seasonal eating frenzy results in weight gain, guilt, self-loathing and even depression. Happy Holidays!

There are varying reports as to how much weight is gained during the holidays. According the New England Journal of Medicine, the real concern is that adults who gain the average one to two pounds during the holidays tend to keep that weight on for life. That means much of midlife weight gain can be explained as holiday eating. The journal sites a study from the Energy Metabolism Lab- USDA Human Nutrition Research center that concludes the news is worse for those who are already over-weight. They tend to gain an average of 5 pounds during the holiday season. These facts may have you already planning a post holiday diet, but why not take a proactive, preventative approach? A study from UCLA indicates the greatest indicator of an adult gaining weight over the next six months is whether or not they have been on a diet in the previous six months. It's a boomerang. This fact has many turning to a new approach.....Conscious Eating.

Conscious eating is also known as intuitive eating, mindful eating, awareness while eating and even eating yoga. What it means in simple terms is paying attention to all dimensions of the food you eat and your eating experience. How do you know if you are conscious? Think of it as the difference between the way you drive normally and the way you drive when a police car is following you. Conscious eating means you fully recognize what, how, when and why you are eating. Dr. Susan Albers defines conscious eating as, "when you learn more about how and why you eat and less about what you eat. When you are so closely in touch with what is going on inside you, you know the exact moment you are satisfied rather than stuffed or starving." The concept of conscious eating is giving rise to "Natural Weight Loss" programs that help people lose weight without counting calories and depriving themselves of the enjoyment of food. These programs teach you to listen to your body versus your mind. Think of it as eating "on purpose."

Try these tips for conscious eating that will guide you through this holiday season:

Intuitive Eating

Make eating a stand-alone activity. Eat at your table or in a pleasing place that makes you smile! Do not eat while working on the computer, watching TV or driving.

Breathe.....before you begin. Taking as little as four deep breaths activates the Vagus nerve which relaxes you, slows down your heart rate and prepares your gastric juices for digestion. It takes the "rush" out of eating.

Look at your food before you eat it. Smell it. Pretend you have never seen this food before. Clear your mind of pre-conceived thoughts of "good food" or "bad food" or "the food you eat" for a particular holiday. Does this food look like you want to eat it? Which smells are appealing? Distinguish as many scents as you can.

Notice if you are really hungry or not. How hungry are you? Is your body telling you this or is it your mind?

If a craving does not come from actual hunger, it will never be satisfied by food.

Chew your food. Buddhism teaches a meditation of chewing every bite 100 times. In our modern world, try 25 times or even 10 times. What texture is the bite? What memories does it evoke? Does it feel good? Savor those traditional holiday foods and remember why you loved them in the first place!

Sip only warm water while you are eating your meal. Warm water aids in digestion. Have that alcoholic drink if you choose during the holidays, but not during the meal. Alcohol numbs us and triggers a sugar craving cycle. We eat more and are less aware of what we are eating while consuming alcohol.

Consider the energy of the food you are eating. You are what you eat. Literally! The food you eat makes up your blood and all your cells. It speaks to your

DNA. What do you want your food to do for you? Root vegetables ground you. Leafy greens lighten you up. Caffeine and alcohol make you tense. Brown rice brings you harmony. How do you want to feel? You are in control.

Modify those beloved holiday recipes. Don't skip the traditions-just make them healthier. Substitute natural sweeteners like agave nectar or brown rice syrup for sugars. Use whole grains like quinoa and kasha instead of white rice and breads. Think of it as a chance to help your entire family get healthier.

Proactively plan for marathon family time. Does your family make the holiday a weekend long event? Over indulging often comes from sheer boredom. If you know you are going to be sitting around for hours on end with nothing else to do but eat....plan to do something else. Bring a good book or game with you. Plan to break up the day with a walk or some stretches. You'll feel better and who knows? Maybe someone else will follow your example.

Enjoy one or two treats! Try decadent, organic dark chocolate....the good stuff. Choose the highest percentage of cocoa (natural chocolate bean) that you can find. Not only is it delicious, it is considered a Super Food for its high anti-oxidant properties. Sorry...regular chocolate chips don't qualify.

CHAPTER 4

Mindful And Gentle Eating Process - How To Interrupt The Pattern Of Emotional Eating

If you're a woman struggling with emotional eating, you probably often feel like you have no control around food. Because you've probably used food for so long to medicate your emotions, it's become second nature. You don't have an accurate picture of it anymore. This is why you probably swear that you can't live without M&Ms, your favorite cheesy puffs or Mom's homemade lasagna. But it's not the food that's hitting your happy spots, it's the connection to those memories. Right now you're linking extreme pleasure to eating the food and the consequence of that is that you can't seem to ever get enough. The truth is you can't get enough of it, because it's not what you really want. You're really seeking the opportunity to re-experience the positive memories that come with eating the food. However in order to extract those feel good feelings, you don't have to overeat the food.

The following method is to be used in conjunction with a permission based eating approach to food called Intuitive Eating. If you are dieting or restricting the foods you eat, you will have a much harder time with this exercise. This is because as a dieter, you will always want what you think you can't have. If you believe that you can't or shouldn't eat chocolate, then it will be extremely difficult for you to feel the level of safety intended in this exercise that comes with knowing that you can eat what you want whenever you get hungry.

In order to fully overcome emotional eating, it is essential that you find resourceful ways of dealing with the often uncomfortable emotions that drive you to eat. It is also important to be able to neutralize these emotions and deal with them so that they do not trigger the desire to overeat. For this, I heartily recommend the use of doing whatever you have to do to cope aggressively with the stress in your life. I teach my clients a variety of techniques listed under the umbrella category of energy psychology tools or energy therapy. They function to eliminate painful emotional and physical blockages in the body. One of my favorite processes is based on the science of acupuncture. It's called Emotional Freedom Technique or EFT.

I've created the following exercise for my Say Goodbye to Dieting Program. I recommend that you use this Mindful and Gentle Eating Exercise to become more conscious of your eating, slow yourself down and refocus on how the food makes you feel and notice how it feels in your body in the moment and over time.

Alisson Pot

The intention of the exercise is to begin to reawaken your sense of how to eat more mindfully, in full conscious awareness of your thoughts and feelings as you eat. If you're inclined to be a fast eater like me, I know how hard it is for you to consider eating more slowly. Eating fast is a sign of compulsion, that stems from fear of lack. Many non diet weight loss programs only advocate eating slowly as a means of breaking the habit of compulsion that drives the speed eating. I don't agree with that. As a gal who has always eaten very fast, I resented it when anyone told me to eat slowly. The resistance you feel is that little survival part of you that refuses to be made to feel unsafe ever again. I promise I won't ever take anything away from you. My only desire is to add to what you already have.

I encourage you to learn by giving you the opportunity to enjoy contrast. I believe that choices are essential to being happy and in order to create new habits effortlessly, you have to feel really good about what you choose. You'll notice in this exercise, I'll ask you to eat slowly and then I'll encourage you to eat at your normal pace, whatever that may be and then alternate between the two speeds. That is done so that your brain can reorganize itself and find an intermediate speed that will become a new comfort level for you. To prepare you to do the exercise, please do the following 5 intermediary steps, A-E.

You may choose to eat anything that you want. The choice is up to you. This exercise is done to consciously slow you down. You may find it a challenge at first, later it will become a great joy.

A. Find five emotional food connections in your life that have in the past compelled you to eat when you were not hungry.

B. What has that food meant to you?

C. What memories rise to the surface when you think about it?

D. Go out and get one of those foods or all of them, bring it home or prepare it. (For best results, you'll practice this exercise each time with each of the individual foods you've chosen)

E. Before you are ready to sit down and eat your chosen food, set your place with the appropriate silverware and a napkin (even if you are eating a pint of ice cream, make sure that you have a napkin) You don't have to serve it in a bowl unless you choose to do so. Now you're ready to begin.

Mindful and Gentle Eating Process

1. Bring your journal to the table
2. Have your silverware and optional plate or bowl ready along with your napkin
3. Place the food on the table

4. Sit down facing it
5. Look at it
6. Smell it
7. Be present with your feelings as they surface
8. Notice those feelings
9. Sit for a few moments and write down your observations of the food and your feelings connected to it
10. Close your journal
11. Pause and think for a moment, offering thanks for this food
12. Pick up your utensil
13. Take a small bite or spoonful.
14. Place the food in your mouth and allow it to rest on the tip of your tongue.
15. Swirl it around in your mouth for about 3 to 7 seconds
16. Notice the sensations that come up for you

17. Slowly chew it or allow it to gently glide down your throat.

18. Put down your fork or spoon and resist picking it up for a moment. If you have to sit on your hands, then do it

19. Just sit with those feelings for about 10 -15 seconds

20. Repeat the process from stage 12-19 until you are satisfied. Notice the degree of that satisfaction. Do this at least 3 times during the week. The rest of the times eat at your normal pace. See what you discover.

TOP 10 TIPS FOR EATING DISORDER RECOVERY - SELF ACCEPTANCE, HEALTH & WELL BEING

I. Work with a treatment team consisting of a therapist, nutritionist, physician and otherprofessionals, if at all possible. Also, seeks out some of the many wonderful self help programs available to assist you in recovery.

Intuitive Eating

Treatment by a team of qualified professionals who specialize in the treatment of anorexia, bulimia, binge eating disorder and/or compulsive overeating is the best course of action to address and recover from disordered eating.

There are highly regarding organizations that offer referrals to treatment professionals available online and by telephone. Consider contacting the National Eating Disorder Association or the Academy of Eating Disorders for a list of professionals who provide treatment in your area. Also, many anorexia, bulimia and BED sufferers and families find that reviewing the online 'virtual brochures' offered in the Eating Disorder Specialist Library greatly simplifies their search for treatment.

If your access to professional treatment is limited, also seek out support through organizations such as Overeaters Anonymous, Eating Disorders

Anonymous, and local church or community groups designed to provide support for sufferers.

II. Develop self acceptance through practicing compassion toward self.

Also, practice kindness toward yourself and offering unconditional self care and self respect. Refuse to allow your self esteem to be determined by outside factors, but rather find your value in the content of your character and by being the uniquely wonderful person God created you to be.

III. Develop a positive and self nurturing internal dialogue.

Our inner dialogue with ourselves is critical to our recovery and general well being. Learn how to recognize ineffective thoughts and replace these with accurate and uplifting thoughts.

IV. Get treatment for co-occurring disorders such as anxiety and depression

Anxiety disorders such as Obsessive Compulsive Disorder (OCD), generalized anxiety, panic disorder, agoraphobia, separation anxiety and social phobias are often co-occurring issues. Learn about the symptoms, treatment and etiology of anxiety disorders and recognize the importance of treating these disorders with therapy and possibly medication, when prescribed by a medical doctor.

V. Practice mindfulness and living in the moment.

Mindfulness is the practice of becoming more aware of the present moment, rather than dwelling in the past or projecting into the future. Many find mindfulness techniques helpful in recovery.

VI. Listen to and honor your feelings.

Feelings matter. Our emotions give us valuable information about ourselves and our perceptions of the environment. Developing awareness of feelings and developing skills to tolerate uncomfortable feelings often go hand in hand with recovery.

VII. Eat well and listen to your body's hunger and fullness signs.

Nutrition is the fuel for our body. Eating disorders often alter what was once a natural and enjoyable relationship with food and our bodies. Learn more about nutrition, intuitive eating and recovery here.

VII. Accept your genetic makeup and appreciate your body.

Body image is our perception of body, not only its appearance, but its functionality, health and purpose. A positive body image is essential to well being and recovery from anorexia, bulimia, and binge eating disorder.

IX. Have a relapse prevention or correction plan.

Learn to recognize the early warning signs of relapse and develop skills and resources to prevent and/or pull oneself out of relapse.

X. Develop faith and trust in God and let go of what you cannot control.

A common trait among sufferers is the obsession with trying to control matters beyond our control. This leads to fear, anxiety and the need to seek comfort inappropriately through disordered eating behaviors.

CHAPTER 5

Mindful And Gentle Eating - The Value Of Slowing Down And Tasting Your Food

If you're a woman who is an emotional eater, you're probably not entirely aware of the fact that your food preferences are based on fulfilling your psychological needs. You are really seeking to re-experience pleasurable memories that come with eating the food you crave. It's true. You like the taste of the food, but what's really driving your compulsion is not the way it tastes, but the way it makes you feel. It's not really Mom's lasagna that you're addicted to, it's the need to feel her close to you. If she was incapable of giving hugs and kisses and she shared her love by feeding you, that's what you crave. If she was a very loving mom who was demonstrative in her affection, you're after that quick hit high that reminds you of those memories that you are lovable. As an emotional eater, you're after the feeling, not the food.

Yet if you've experienced the fall out that comes with years of dieting, you've been led to believe that you have no control around food. That's not true. But since you're so used to being deprived, you've lost sight of your natural, innate ability to be a picky eater. However you can learn to free yourself of the ties that bind you to emotional eating and become a very discriminating eater.

Perhaps you're making the common mistake that I did thinking that you're just a human garbage can, devouring anything in sight. That's not true. That's only a response to feeling deeply deprived, feeling fearful and guilty about wanting what you think you shouldn't be eating. That comes from years of dieting that monkeys with your brain, throwing all your safety switches out of whack. Despite the harm that dieting has done, you can still reverse it by making the choice to say goodbye to dieting. It's never too late to learn how to make peace with food and stop fearing it. When you learn to become a more mindful eater, you'll be more sensitive to appreciate the many wonderful nuances of the food you eat. I created a technique called the Mindful and Gentle Eating Process. I teach it to my clients and recommend that they use it in conjunction with a permission based approach to eating such as the process called Intuitive Eating. Then to stack the odds in your favor, I encourage you to combine the technique with a commitment to taking a proactive stance towards dealing with the stress in your life. By doing this, your response to food will begin to change. You will no longer crave many of the foods you eat, because you'll notice that they are often bland and tasteless, mediocre at best.

Intuitive Eating

The following story demonstrates my application of the Mindful and Gentle Eating Process that I created. If you haven't already tried the process, give it a go and see how it works for you. Here's how it worked for me.

There's a message in my apple sauce. One day I woke up early in the morning, around 5:00 a.m., actually feeling very hungry, or so I thought. For the past several months, I've gotten into a comfortable pattern where I tend not to eat breakfast until about 11:30. Back in the days when I was dieting, that was absolutely unheard of, I was always starving as soon as I woke up. Now I can go for hours without the first glimmer of hunger.

But today seemed different. I was hungry so I went downstairs to the kitchen and chose some Mott's Cinnamon Applesauce from the refrigerator and spooned a few tablespoons into a small dish. Feeling a bit pressured to get my day started and finally finish the editing on my book; without even tasting the applesauce, I ate the first bite very quickly with a kind of desperation. Then I noticed that I was really anxious and felt very pressured to finish the book. Separating myself from that urgency for a moment, I wondered what would happen if I ate the next bite more slowly. I noticed that my thoughts instantly changed their quality and began to slow down as I began to more consciously and slowly savor the taste of the applesauce from the spoon. I noticed it was more tart than I would have liked.

As I sat there in a bit of daze, I asked myself, "Why do I want this now? It's not even that good. It's been so long that I've had an early breakfast, why now and what does this applesauce remind me of?

Then it hit me as I looked into the dish and saw the applesauce, it was almost as though I was being transported back in time to my Nana's kitchen long ago, sitting at the sparkling white kitchen table, looking at all the apples on the counter top and enjoying the wafting scent and the wonderful aromas of the cinnamon and apples gently simmering on the stove top for fresh pies and apple sauce.

I went a bit deeper into the memory and could see the patterned wall paper adorning the kitchen walls and feel the cool, hard flooring under my feet. I could even visualize sitting in my favorite chair looking across the small kitchen out the window at the magnificent view of the Hudson River and the majestic New York City skyline. I watched the cars rolling over the George Washington Bridge. I could even see my Nana, all smiles in her frilly apron as she peeled and cut the apples with her deft fingers moving so quickly. I even could make out the details of her wedding ring.

Caught in my reverie, I had one more spoonful of applesauce and realized that I no longer wanted it. I took the rest and put it away for later. I knew that the applesauce had already done its job. It brought me back to a place where I remembered feeling such love and warmth and being happy. I adored my Nana.

Ok. Let me explain what I'd like you to take away from this story. Different foods have different associations in your brain. This is why you get cravings for certain foods. You are actually craving the emotion that the food holds from the memories that are connected to the food. If you are emotional eater, food has more meanings and connections for you than people who don't feel so attached to eating.

When you take an extra moment and linger over the food and ask yourself what it reminds you of, you are putting yourself in a position of being an observer. You are no longer unconscious of what you are doing.

Intuitive Eating

It is when we are unaware of what we are eating that we eat more because we don't experience the satisfaction that comes from the enjoyment of the food.

What do you think of slowing down and noticing what you are reminded of today when you eat your food. Who knows, like me, it may change the flavor completely and you may need to just sit in silence for a few minutes and really let those memories seep into your soul and enjoy knowing that they will live in your heart forever. Remember it's not the food you're seeking, it's the feeling. Go for the feelings. Notice what you are feeling. Amazing things will come of it.

As a post script, I notice that I don't feel the same degree of tension that I did before to finish the editing on my book. As a result, the irritation that I had over some other things going on in my life has also lifted significantly. In fact, since I'm exploring how I feel, I realize that I'm still tired and I'm going back to sleep. I attribute this newfound relaxation to my being able to reconnect to the memories of how my Nana approached life, one step at a time. Boy that morning applesauce had a lot more than I expected.

CHAPTER 6

The Secret To Ending Emotional Eating

Are you an emotional eater? Want to know an important secret?

Stop searching for that one magical diet that is going to set you free because it doesn't exist!

If you're an emotional eater, there isn't a diet on earth that's going to work for you.

Trust me. It it had existed I would have found it. I spent decades reading about and trying more diets than I care to admit.

I jumped from diet to diet to diet, looking for the magic mix of foods and rules to melt away the excess pounds. When I finally understood that no such diet exists, I felt my whole body relax and my relationship with food begin to change.

Diets are not designed to deal with emotional eating. If you're an emotional eater going on a diet to lose weight is like trying to open a lock with the wrong key!

Why Diets Don't Work for Emotional Eating

Diets address the physical; not the mental; not the emotional. And as women, we are emotional creatures.

Have you noticed what happens when you try to solve emotional eating issues with dieting? You may lose some weight for a while, but it always comes back. Why? Because you are focusing on a symptom - your weight; not the cause, which is how you are using food.

When you are stuck in this cycle it's like being caught in a trap. Then when you finally realize what you've been doing, its like being set free. It's so exhilarating you want to jump up and down and scream and let every other woman in the universe in on the SECRET! You want to shout, "Stop. Stop. I've discovered the truth. Stop torturing yourself. Take this key and set yourself free."

It's not the food that's the problem. It's your inappropriate use of food that's the problem. Confusing the two will make you crazy.

Dealing with Emotional Eating

Begin to focus on the real issue, which isn't your weight. It's the feelings and stresses that cause you to seek comfort in food. I know it's scary, but that is where you need to focus your attention because then food begins to lose its power over you.

Alisson Pot

Figure out what you are really craving. When you find yourself standing in front of the open refrigerator ready to chow down on that leftover cake or chinese food (like I was tempted to do recently) pause and ask yourself, "Am I really hungry?" If not, put the food back, close the refrigerator door and ask yourself what's really going on? Are you bored? Are you lonely? Are you anxious? Are you angry?

Filling up with food when you really need a hug, a friend, a new job, someone to listen to you, is only going to make matters worse. Because you know what comes next - anger, disgust and self recrimination.

No amount of chocolate or ice cream can fix emotional emptiness. (And stuffing yourself full of vegetables or brown rice till you burst isn't the answer either.)

Intuitive Eating

Don't get me wrong. I love chocolate and ice cream. But I prefer to indulge for enjoyment when I'm happy, not as a coping mechanism that I'll regret later.

As my favorite teacher loves to say, "Don't eat to get happy. Get happy and then eat."

It's not always easy.

You know how it goes. A stressful day at the office or argument with your husband sends you to the nearest drive-through.

If it's any consolation. You're not alone. Science is beginning to show that women, in particular, are more susceptible to eating when stressed. Emotions can trigger physical hunger through the mood and appetite regulation chemicals in your brain. It's not about lack of willpower. Your brain and body are trying to achieve chemical balance.

When you have a terrible day, your brain's production of serotonin (a neurotransmitter that keeps you from feeling anxious and depressed) can drop, leading to irritability and increased appetite.

To maintain its proper levels, your brain wants carbohydrates, to help replace serotonin. That's why, after an intense day at the office, you crave pizza or pasta, not grilled chicken and steamed broccoli. Low serotonin can also impair your ability to tell when you're full, making you more likely to eat when you don't really need to as well as more prone to overeating.

Knowing what's going on with your brain and body can make it easier to adjust your behaviors and go easy on yourself.

Begin with Understanding and Self Kindness

Intuitive Eating

Be gentle with yourself. Stop beating yourself up. It's much easier to change your behavior from a place of understanding and compassion.

You didn't get to where you are right now overnight and you are not going to heal yourself overnight. That's okay.

It takes time and practice, but you can change the way you react. You can train yourself to seek healthier comforts and/or distract yourself until the cravings subside. Expect setbacks. I've been working on this for years and there still are times when I end up off course. The past two weeks are a great example. I've been staying with my Mom, whose mom just died and my Dad who has Alzheimer's Disease, in a house loaded with every trigger food imaginable.

Fortunately once you've discovered instinctive/intuitive eating, you tend not to stray too far for too long. It's too uncomfortable. You want to get back on track. And maybe once in a while you may need to experience the discomfort of overeating to remember how wonderful it feels to eat when you're hungry and stop when you're full.

CHAPTER 7

Eating Rules To Follow To Lose Weight And Body Fat

Let's be honest with ourselves, for some of us, losing weight is like pushing a boulder up a steep hill. We may make a little progress by depriving ourselves of certain foods, trying a crazy new popular fad diet, or even flat out starving ourselves, but once we slip and the sense of failure sets in... the boulder slides downwards and we pack on a few extra pounds for the effort. It is frustrating, and I know the feeling all too well.

However, I think it is important not to deprive ourselves completely from something as wonderful as our favorite foods, but rather guide ourselves in a way where we can have the best of both worlds. We may want to enjoy our favorites all the time... but we also do have a weight loss goal that we are trying to achieve.

So here are three rules to keep in mind and to follow to lose weight:

1. Favorites are not Forbidden - Don't deprive yourself of your favorite foods because the whiplash of your cravings are going to do more damage than good. It really just comes down to... eat your favorites; just not every day. For instance, have the sausage you love one day and turkey sausage or turkey bacon the rest of the week.

2. Eat Nutritiously - There are a lot of foods out there that have hardly any nutrients in them at all and are just high empty calories (mind you they may taste great, but they are just going to add to your thighs and belly). So learn to choose foods with high nutrient densities and fewer calories. For example, a slice of

white bread versus whole wheat bread; where whole wheat bread would give you 2 g of fiber, and white may not even give you 1 g.

3. Eat More Food (Don't Diet) - Now this may be counter intuitive... eat more food to lose weight? Well, when you eat balanced meals throughout the day; you are more likely to be full, and there will be less chances of you having gorging sessions in the evening. For instance, if you had a large plate of pasta for dinner, you will probably find yourself still hungry, and heading over for seconds or thirds. Now, on the other hand if you had grilled chicken salad with a bit of pasta in it and some fruit for dessert, you will probably find yourself better off nutrient wise, calorie wise, and full (for a longer period).

CHAPTER 8

Don't Stop Eating Fat To Lose Weight

It's a little counter intuitive. Eat more fat and lose more weight? Isn't it the other way around? That would make sense but studies show that as a whole, although we are consuming much less fat than 30 years ago, we're still gaining more weight. Let's take a look at the this phenomena a little closer.

A Drop in Fat Consumption?

In 1978, about 40% of American were getting their calories from fat. This meant a higher consumption of meat, butter, cheese, whole milk and other foods high in fat. Then about 10 years later, the fat consumption dropped about 10% to 34% of American Diet came from fat calories. This number declined just a little bit further to 33% ten years after that in 1996. Now about 30% is the recommended maximum for the amount of calories coming from fat. So as a whole, America is pretty healthy nearly following the recommended guidelines right? WRONG!

But Why Are We Still Fat?

There are two things to blame as to why America's fat consumption decreased but more and more Americans were getting fatter. First, the way that the consumption data was gathered was deemed to be a little faulty. But the main reason is that although American's percentage of calories from fat went down, the total amount of calorie consumption went up by 7% between the late 70s and late 90s.

We're Consuming Too Many Calories

This is like saying I ate a 500 calorie meal during lunch (say a salad) and I used this dressing that accounted for 40% of the total calories for this meal.

Say I used 200 calories worth of dressing and it was purely fat. Then, to continue the example, I ate a 600 calorie salad for dinner and used the same amount of dressing (i.e. 200 calories). Now, for dinner my total fat calories was still 200 calories like it was for lunch. But, in total, I had more calories during dinner. So the net effect is that I am still having too many calories, although my total fat calories appears to be less of the percentage I had during lunch.

Now when you add the increase of calories to the fact that 30% of men and 45% of women say they rarely or never exercise, it's no wonder why 65% of Americans are considered to by overweight or obese today compared to the 20% in 1977.

CHAPTER 9

How To Lose Weight By Eating For Energy

Are you bewildered when intuitive eating guides tell you to eat when you're hungry and stop when you're full? It can be a difficult skill to relearn after years of dieting and/or bingeing. One entirely different way to eat the right amount for your body is to change the goal from "getting full of food" to "eating for energy".

Food is fuel, but that sounds so sterile. A more exciting and empowering approach is to eat feel great. Eat until you feel light and full of energy. When you use this method, you don't even have to think about the amount of food in your stomach.

When you sit down to eat; ask your body to let you know when it has had enough. Pay close attention with each bite. You will get a subtle, but clear, message to stop when your body has had enough. You may even think you're making it up. The message will often come after just a small amount of food.

When you experiment by following your "full" signal and stop eating at that point, you will find yourself feeling light and energized. You may not even feel a difference in your stomach at all.

Make it a practice to give your body just what it needs...not too much...not too little.

As you eat, ask yourself if you need more energy...

* Will you feel better, lighter, more energized if you eat this bite?

* Will you feel comfortable and satisfied?

* Or will you feel heavy, tired, too full?

Intuitive Eating

The body has amazing powers of self-regulation and will communicate its needs to you if you will listen.

At first it may feel strange to eat this way. Over time though, you will find that...

* Your energy levels are soaring.

* You are not getting sleepy after you eat.

* You feel less fuzzy.

* You feel more replenished by food.

* Fresh, unprocessed foods become more and more appealing to you and make you feel better.

* You are more creative.

* You feel happier and more at peace with yourself.

* Extra pounds have dropped away easily and effortlessly.

Alisson Pot

In the beginning it may seem like paying so much attention to your hunger and energy takes a lot of time and attention. Just remember that the skills you're learning will set you free from obesity and diet craziness for the rest of your life.

CHAPTER 10

Calorie Reality---Eating Healthier But Still Gaining Weight

Are you choosing healthier, more nutrient dense foods and discovering a few extra pounds?

Organic, natural and "back to earth" foods are on the rise. Unfortunately, weight gain is too. According to the Center for Disease control, the average weight for men in 1960 was 166.3 pounds and the average weight for women was 140 pounds. In 2002 the average weight for men rose to 191 pounds and to 164.3 pounds for women. If there has been an increasing effort to eat healthier, what seems to be the reason(s) for these statistics?

Contradicting information on what is healthy and which weight loss philosophies work the best may be a contributing factor in weight gain. Low-Carb, high protein, glycemic index, blood type, acid-base, hormone, food-combinations, sugar busting, volumizing, metabolic, intuitive eating are all terms that you have come across in the media. What a head spinning flurry of words and philosophies. Where is one to turn? What works best? The truth is any one of these methods can work for weight loss. The question is--- which one will work for you over the long run? Any diet that cuts back on calories will bring about slight weight loss. Keeping the weight off is a whole other episode. Remember, the body recognizes a calorie as a unit of energy no matter where that calorie might come from. People are smarter in changing their eating habits today and including more whole grains, healthy fats and complex carbohydrates. The information that is accessible via the web and from the government is continuously becoming more reliable. That may explain part of the recent upward trend in the purchasing of whole, organic and natural foods. Sales in these areas are increasing at alarming rates. So why are you still not accomplishing your goal of weight loss? Let's examine some healthy food choices that are also the culprits of added calories.

Nuts:

Packed with fiber, protein, and various minerals and vitamins the nut family can supply up to 205 calories per ounce. That is the amount in 24 small almonds, seven shelled walnuts and less than a quarter cup of cashews. Try using nuts on salads, in sandwich fillings or eat out of the shell to keep the portion size under control. Remember to buy them raw and roast yourself to save on fat and added calories.

Granola:

Wow, talk about a knockout blow. One cup can supply somewhere in the neighborhood of 550 calories. The trick is to use a very small amount with your yogurt, as a dessert topping, in parfaits, or as part of a trail mix for those long fall hikes. Most granola cereals are high in fiber, protein and potassium and usually contain a high amount of fat. Choose lower fat versions like Quaker.

Protein Bars:

Decisions, decisions, decisions--- look at all the brands on the shelves today. This highly marketed product is showing up everywhere in all shapes and sizes. The problem with this is the calorie, fat and sugar amount included. It may be wiser (for your waistline) to choose a good old Snicker's bar at 280 calories instead of some whopping 420 calorie high protein "bulking" bar. There are also a lot of added ingredients in these bars like sugar alcohols and fractionated oils. Choose low-calorie, low fat bars that include five grams of fiber or more for a great filling snack.

Dried Fruits:

Dried means the water was extracted out of the product along with most of the vitamin C. The natural sugar is concentrated due to the dehydration status---this means you have to eat more to get a sufficient volume. Shelf life is increased and the flavor is more concentrated. Read the food label and ingredient list carefully for added ingredients. A small serving of dried bananas chips contains 218 calories and 14 grams of fat. The fat comes from the added coconut oil. That very small red box of raisins has 130 calories inside. Premium tropical pineapples contain 140 calories for one-third cup and 16 grams of sugar (sugar is the second ingredient listed). Use a small amount of dried fruit products on salads or with string cheese as a balanced snack.

Fruit Juices:

Sugar, sugar everywhere--- reading the front of the container will leave you feeling like you are the healthiest person in the world for drinking juice. You will see a variety of health claims on the front. Read the label and the ingredient list to assure you are choosing the right product. Fruit juices are all sugar and carbohydrates. They do not include any fats or protein into your diet. Look for 100% fruit juice products and limit them to no more than six ounces per day. A four ounce serving contains 55 calories and 12 grams of sugar. Also, take a look at those sport drinks. A typical bottle contains 200 calories, 56 grams of carbohydrates and 440 grams of sodium. "Eat the whole fruit and nothing but the fruit."

Including healthier foods into your diet for optimum nutrition is something everyone should look at increasing. These healthy choices should not be piled on top of your current intake; they should replace foods that are nutrient poor. For managing your weight you should always keep focus on the food label and the ingredient list. Portion sizes should be the focus, like any other food choice, when adding these high calorie nutrient dense foods.

weight loss foods: 5 worst foods to eat to lose weight

One of the most effective methods to lose weight seems a little counter intuitive: eat more. By increasing the frequency of the meals that you take in, you can increase your body's metabolism to improve your body's ability to gain nutrition out of food and naturally burn fat. Your body stores fat as a reserve for energy which can be used later and it does this very effectively; one pound of fat contains approximately 3500 calories. A combination of the right food, light to intensive exercise, and proper rest is an excellent way to lose weight.

If we look at the foods we eat closely we find that most provide the wrong nutritional values to someone trying to lose weight. Unfortunately, it is usually the great tasting foods that are the culprits of unwanted weight gain. Fast food is the most readily accessible food but it is loaded with calories which, when taken in excess, will be preserved by your body in the form of fat.

Everyone has different rates of metabolism which can be calculated using formulas to determine the persons basal metabolic rate (BMR) using the person's weight, height, and age. From here we can have a rough idea of just how many calories we should ideally consume at the maximum. Case in point: an average sized woman with a BMR of 1267 kcal per day should not consume one meal that supplies her with her daily requirement as this will make her metabolic rate very sluggish. She will need to spread out her meals to remain healthy, preferably between 4 and 6 meals.

The worst foods for weight loss include those that have excessive amounts of the gluten protein found in food manufactured from rye, wheat, and barley. Most carbohydrate rich foods which have hard to digest sugars can cause weight gain--avoid the 'king sized' burgers! Number two of the worst foods is cola based drinks; just 12 ounces of the stuff amounts to 150 calories. Third, and the most common, is potato chips. These culprits are used in many informal occasions, too much of it and your waist line pays the price. Fourth and a particular favorite with women are the chocolate based cookies; these normally have hydrogenated oils which are not good for someone on a diet. The fifth is the full fat cheeses; these are made with saturated fat and contain about

10grams of fat per ounce. Today there exist healthy alternatives to these food types, and as someone losing weight, you should consult with a nutritionist about the options available to you.

INTUITIVE FITNESS - 7 STEPS TO GET YOUR "GUT" IN GEAR

The best way to finally gain control over your weight, your fitness and your health is not through dieting, it's not through starvation or overtraining, it's deciding once and for all to use your inherent Intuitive ability (your "GUT" instincts) and work in conjunction with your body...Instead of against it!! As a former Fitness Instructor and personal trainer for over 30 years, I have seen one gimmick after another come into the Health & Fitness Industry with its promises of rapid weight loss and false fitness claims. You have ultimate control over making the changes you want to make. But... you must take a different approach from a different perspective, to get permanent results. In this chapter, I will briefly outline the steps you can take today to get the results you desire... the results YOU deserve! So....Let's get your "gut" in gear! Your Gut Instincts....that is!

Step 1: Ask your body what it needs - Go into a state of relaxation either sitting quietly or in meditation and with your Intuitive Mind, ask what your body needs... and then listen. Use the power of your Intuition your "gut instincts" Write it down. We have lost connection with our bodies it's time to reconnect!

Step 2: Tell your body what you want - Visualize & Feel your ideal body...Every night before you go to sleep and every morning the minute you wake up and as much as you can during the day... get a good visual of what you want your body to look and feel like. And act as if it has already happened.

Step 3: Balance - This is nature's scale. Our bodies are amazing works of both Art & Science. An amazing system of biological Intelligence that does exactly what nature calls for. Treat your Body as the intelligent system that it is. Overdoing anything is not good practice. Eat with balance in mind. Put "good" energetic thoughts into what you eat. If you tend to be hungry all time, eat more nutritious foods. Your body is trying to tell you it's starving. Starving for nutrition that is.

Step 4: Water - You've heard it 100 times, did you really listen? I struggle with this one myself. But, water is a critical element-literally and our bodies need it to run efficiently. Any perceived lack in the body triggers "starvation programs" within the body. These need to be reset. This is what we are trying to accomplish by following the steps outlined. Once the programs are reset, your weight or more importantly your health becomes much easier to maintain.

Step 5: Eat Live Foods - Our bodies are living, breathing systems that hold our "life force" it requires "life force" from foods to function optimally. Can you "survive" on junk food? Sure you can but, for how long? We are poisoning our bodies with chemicals, which throw our systems more out of balance chemically. - We are talking about a literal chemical reaction in the body that keeps "fat" from being utilized properly. Our bodies actually 'hold on" to that fat and so the cycle continues. If you really listen to your body intuitively, you would change immediately what foods you put into it. Feed your body fresh fruits, vegetables, Nuts etc. for the life force they provide. Juicing is an excellent source of life force. Try a little wheatgrass while you're at it!

Step 6: Get Moving! - that seems pretty intuitive doesn't it? Our bodies need exercise. But exercise in balance. Walking everyday for 30-40 minutes is all you really need. I like to carry a set of hand weights to provide a little resistance as well for the muscles. Your body is pure energy, it needs to take on and release energy to stay in balance. Now that's a nice way to view it... isn't it? Pretty simple and intuitive!

Step 7: Herbs, oils, salt baths - To de-stress and re-connect with our bodies try salt baths with herbs and oils of your choosing. Stress keeps the "fat program" ON. This is an excellent way to turn it OFF.

DISCOVER GUILT-FREE EATING - STOP BEATING YOURSELF UP

How do you talk to yourself? Do you ever listen to what you say? Everyday, you have hundreds of thoughts going on in your head, many about yourself.

Stop and listen sometime. Would you talk to a child the way you talk to yourself? Chances are you would deeply hurt a child and lower his or her self-esteem with the things you say to yourself.

The Challenge

So why do you talk to yourself that way? It's probably a habit by now, second nature. What has this kind of talk done to your self-esteem? I can hear it now, "I'm too fat", "I can't believe I broke down and ate that cookie, what is wrong with me?", "I will never lose this weight", "I don't deserve it", and on and on. You don't need anyone else to say mean things to you and lower your self-esteem, you do a good job yourself.

The fact is that self-esteem is related to what you eat and what you weigh. How is this possible? Look at the results you are getting (or not getting) right now. Then look at the way you talk and feel about yourself. These negative thoughts are creating your reality.

Here is how it works: our thoughts lead to beliefs which lead to behavior which lead to results.

Go back and read that last sentence again. Memorize it and say it to yourself often. If you aren't getting the results you want, change your thoughts.

For example, here is a person who talks to themselves in a negative manner:

Thought: "I am fat"

Belief: "It doesn't matter what I eat, I'll never lose the weight"

Behavior: "I might as well eat the whole box of cookies"

Result: "Weight gain"

Can you identify with this type of conversation? Do you see how starting out with a negative thought can ultimately lead to a negative result?

The Solution

You need to start with a positive thought to remove the shame and guilt and start boosting your self-esteem. Then you can eat without guilt, enjoy the food, and reach your goals.

Let's take a look at how positive thinking can dramatically change your result:

Thought: "I am thin and fit!"

Belief: "If I eat based on my body's needs, I will achieve my body's healthy weight"

Behavior: "I can enjoy one cookie, and I know that all foods in moderation can be part of a healthy lifestyle"

Result: "Each day I am closer to my body's healthy weight!"

It may not be easy for you to change those negative thoughts, but as you start thinking positively, you will be able to make better eating choices, and this will help you to achieve your body's natural, healthy weight (without strict dieting or deprivation!)

DISCOVER GUILT-FREE EATING: FEEL YOUR FEELINGS

Are you stuffing your feelings down with food? In other words, when you get stressed, frustrated, angry or depressed do you find yourself eating rather than dealing with the circumstances that are causing you to feel a certain way?

Don't beat yourself up if you are doing this. You're certainly not alone. Not only are millions of people doing the same thing, but I've been there too.

Challenge

We don't start out in life eating for emotional reasons. It's actually something we learn. As we grow up we learn not to trust our body to tell us when to eat. Emotional eating is usually taught by our parents or other authority figures. What happened when you fell down and hurt yourself? Did you get a cookie "to make it better"?

In our society, we also associate holidays, birthdays, and almost any event with food. We eat for almost any reason - stress, anger, sadness, boredom, happiness, excitement, just about anything but physical hunger.

Do you ever crave "comfort food"? This is usually a sign that you are experiencing some kind of intense emotion. You may not even realize this if you often engage in emotional overeating. Comfort food allows us to "stuff down" those feelings and "numb out" temporarily from the feeling.

Food is a distraction and when you overeat so much that you feel sick, this creates an even bigger distraction. If you can relate to this, don't beat yourself up. Like me, this is how you learned to take care of yourself, it's a protective measure. You could have learned to use drugs, alcohol, shopping, gambling, or any other destructive habit instead of using food.

Solution

There is good and bad news. First, the bad news - you will have to feel your feelings. The good news is as you truly allow yourself to feel your feelings, they will lower in intensity and so will the desire for comfort food.

Of course there is a good chance you won't know what you are feeling. This is because food is usually the response to any intense feeling. So first, you need to be aware of when you are going for food. If you find you really aren't physically hungry, ask yourself what you're feeling. This isn't always so simple, especially when you do not want to face the truth of the issue. Run through a list of emotions - anxious, lonely, bored, tired, angry, hurt, embarrassed?

If you can't identify the feeling, that's ok. Keep trying and practicing as feelings come up. Journaling thoughts and feelings is very helpful for some people to identify what emotion is going on.

If you can determine the feeling, ask yourself, "Am I going to die if I sit with this feeling for five minutes?" All you have to do is sit and feel. It may not feel very good, but notice how it gets less intense as you allow yourself to feel it. As you practice this more and more, you will find it easier to deal with emotions and find yourself less drawn to food to solve your problems.

HOW TO STOP EATING BY EXPERIENCING ENOUGH

Do you ever have the sense that you just can't quit eating? That there is never enough? That you are a bottomless pit? These experiences are an opportunity to look deeper, to find out what may be going on behind it.

Don't blame your food or weight. Allow yourself to look deeper. You may discover that this sense of not getting enough permeates your life.

You may find you live life from an inner sense of poverty, a deep down sense of lack that virtually guarantees no amount of food will satisfy you. That no amount of friends, sex, clothes, or money will satisfy you.

Intuitive Eating

When you look closer, you may find that feeling deprived of food today can be based on a very real experience of having been deprived in the past.

Consider a child who couldn't get enough of her mother's love. There is nothing the child can do about this. But as an adult, she is in control of how much food she could eat. So she eats more to make up for not having had enough of something vital in her past, in this case, love.

Feeling deprived of love can also have the opposite effect when the desire to feel loved is so overwhelming that a person shuts down, and ends up restricting food intake. They are, in effect, clamping down on food in order to keep the overwhelming desire for love and connection under control.

To heal this emotional overeating (or under-eating) begin to look for proof in your life that there is enough. We all have places in our lives where we experience enough-ness.

We all have signals in our lives that there is enough. How does your body signal that it has had enough of a good time at a party, and that it is time to go? How does your body signal that I it has had enough of shopping, and needs a break? How does your body tell you, "Enough of the computer already, let's do something else!"?

As you are able to notice your body's "enough" signals, begin to tune into those signals around food and eating. For instance, the body signals that you have eaten enough food by feelings of satisfaction or fullness. Slow down while you are eating and look for those signals.

Remember, if you are distracted, for instance, watching TV or playing on the computer while eating, it will be difficult to notice the signal. Also, if you are limiting your food intake, or judging yourself, it will be very difficult to notice the signal.

When you allow yourself free access to food without judgment and tune into yourself, you can begin to move past deprivation. And while that can feel terrifying, as you learn to re-connect with your signals of hunger and satiety, you will learn that you are not insatiable. That there is enough.

Amazingly, paying attention to self-care around food and far-reaching benefits. As you re-connect with hunger and satiety, you will separate out eating from the emptiness of not feeling loved. You will then have an opportunity to heal from not feeling loved. As you quit blaming your food and your body, you discover you are enough.

STOP TRYING TO CONTROL HOW YOU EAT AND TAKE CHARGE INSTEAD

Taking charge of how you eat allows you to make the choices that are right for you. Being in control has negative connotations and sometimes may mean forcing yourself to do something you don't necessarily want to do. Being in control means using willpower and determination even if that choice isn't right for you. Being in charge means being mindful of what your body needs in any given situation and making the choice based on what is right for you at the time.

It allows you to totally tune into your body's needs and not be affected by outside influences. Making choices because that's what you need not what you should do or have. Accordingly, tuning in to your body's natural instincts by eating naturally is sustainable long term. When you learn to love and trust yourself you choose healthy options more often as you feel more vibrant, have more energy and love being fit and healthy.

When you are in charge sometimes the right choice for you at the time might be overeating. However, when you are listening you can feel the consequences of that choice, reflect on it and perhaps make a different choice next time. It's about loving and respecting yourself. We are all different, we all have different tastes, wants and needs around food. That's why Natural Eating works because it doesn't matter what our gender, race, age, height, build or environment is. We can all simply eat what we want when we are hungry and stop when we are satisfied.

Most of my clients eat healthy nutritious food most of the time. However the problem is that because it is healthy they tend to overindulge reasoning that they can have as much as they like simply because it is healthy. However because our stomachs are only about the size of our fist they don't hold very much without stretching and being uncomfortable. Often we have got into the habit of eating a certain amount. Once we are aware of that and can focus on what our body is telling us, we will eat only the amount we need.

Accordingly, we start eating smaller amounts more frequently. This means we are never depriving ourselves, we're always satisfied, our blood sugar levels are balanced and we feel great. We choose predominantly healthy food because that's what our body tends to want, but we choose to eat unhealthy food if that's what we need at the time. Again by truly listening to our body we will only eat small amounts of the unhealthy food as we don't feel good if you have large amounts of fat, sugar and salt.

Being in charge empowers you to make positive choices that are right for you. Remember the right choice could be a chocolate bar but if you are truly listening it would probably only be a small one.

HOW TO EAT NATURALLY ANYWHERE, ANYTIME

What I love about natural eating is that absolutely anyone can do it. It doesn't matter whether you are a 6 foot 4 inch male doing manual work all day long, or a 5 foot 4 inch woman, running your own business or something of a sedentary nature. Because the principles are the same it doesn't matter what the situation is. You simply listen to your body so you can:

1. Eat when you are hungry
2. Eat exactly what you want
3. Stop when you are satisfied
4. Do something else after eating.

So naturally an active adult male is going to eat a larger portion size and possibly more often than a sedentary women, but they still both follow the above principles based on their needs. Because natural eating is all about how we eat and not what we eat, anyone can do it as long as they are mindful. Here are some guidelines to help you over the holiday period:

1. Focus on the event, not the food. Enjoy catching up with friends, colleagues and family. Yes there will probably be food and drink everywhere you go. If you are hungry have something to eat, simply eat it mindfully so you know when to stop.

2. If food is being passed around, place some on a serviette or plate so you know how much you are having. If you finish what you have and you are still hungry, you can always get more. However if you just

keep eating as it is passed round it is very easy to overeat without being aware of it.

3. Don't eat when you are not hungry so as not to offend anyone. You can always decline politely or ask if you can take some with you or perhaps have it a bit later when you are hungry.

4. Don't starve yourself all day so you can eat heaps when you go out. Our body hates it and you are slowing your metabolism down. Simply eat small amounts regularly as your body asks for it.

5. Similarly if you know you are going to a function where food and drink will be available and you are hungry before you go, don't have a huge meal just as you are setting off. This means you won't be hungry and won't be able to join in with everyone else. Simply have a small snack to take the edge off and then you can enjoy the food available when you get there.

6. Eat exactly what you want every day, then the holidays are no different. So many of us are spending so much time eating what we should that when the holidays come around or a special function like a birthday, we are naturally going to overindulge.

7. If you are going out for the day to the beach or park etc, take plenty of food with you so you can have what you like when you are hungry. If you get over hungry or have to settle for something you don't like, it is so easy to overeat.

I love catching up with friends and family and yes thoroughly enjoy the yummy food which I probably don't have every day. However, I still eat in the same way. If I'm hungry I eat exactly what I feel like and when I've had enough I stop. The difference is it is very easy for me to stop because it doesn't matter what I am eating and how good it tastes, when I've had enough that's it. I also know I can eat exactly what I like any time and actually I'll be hungry again in a very short time anyway.

So it's all a matter of being mindful of what your body is telling you, being prepared and trusting yourself to make the right decisions for you at that time, no matter what is going on around you.

DO THIS MINDFUL EATING TECHNIQUE FOR EASY WEIGHT LOSS

Hold your horses. Slow down!

It's a long and forgotten theme in today's fast paced society. Our lacking ability to slow down is causing devastating health effects in our population especially with the way we eat.

Personally, I have seen numerous people wolfing down their food like there is no tomorrow. We eat like we've been starving for days, or its our last meal on Earth! One of the most distinguishable characteristics of our inability to slow down when we eat, is the rapidly increasing rate of obesity.

Obesity is at an all time high of almost 36%, and almost 70% of Americans are overweight-with similar rates around the world (Center for Disease Control). It has been proven scientifically that eating fast increases our risk for becoming overweight.

So, why does eating fast make us overweight?

1. We cannot gauge how biologically hungry we are!

Oftentimes we will eat far beyond what we should because we ate too fast. How many of you have eaten a large amount of food and not realized you were overfull until about 10 minutes after? Probably every single one of us.

Intuitive Eating

There is a slight lag between how full we are in our stomach, and to how quickly that is communicated to our brain. By eating too fast, we don't give our stomach adequate time to communicate how full we are to our brain.

2. Eating too fast doesn't allow us to enjoy the dining experience, which is essential to not overeating!

Our brain needs the psychological satisfaction from eating. Shoving food down your throat doesn't let you sit back and enjoy the rush of serotonin and other 'feel good' hormones and chemicals that your body releases into your blood stream.

We thrive off these feelings, and if you rush through your meal, you don't get to enjoy them as easily. Your brain will be left psychologically dissatisfied and be craving more food because of it.

With that said, it's very difficult to slow down, when our minds are racing at 100 miles an hour and we are constantly thinking about other things like work, who is babysitting the kids this weekend, and other issues that occupy our day-to-day life

But if we apply just a little bit of effort we can do it, and help shed a few extra pounds.

Try These Hacks...

#1: Set down your utensil in between each bite of food.

#2: Chew each bite of food 20-30 times.

#3: Don't have distractions like TV when you eat.

Try these out. I can guarantee you that this will be very difficult to do, but if you can consistently implement this strategy, you will lose weight naturally!

HOW TO HONE YOUR INTUITION

"The intuitive mind is a sacred gift and the rational mind is a faithful servant. We have created a society that honors the servant and has forgotten the gift."
~Albert Einstein

Many of our society's most successful people - from Bill Gates to Oprah Winfrey to Albert Einstein - have stressed the importance of intuition and have depended on it in their personal and professional lives. As Albert Einstein explained intuition is a sacred gift that we are each bestowed with.

What is intuition? Intuition is the culmination of various instantaneous mental processes including: automatic processing, subliminal priming, implicit memory, heuristics, right-brain processing, instant emotions, nonverbal communication and creativity. As As Dr. Joyce Brothers advises "Trust your hunches. They're usually based on facts filed away just below the conscious level."

Your intuition or knowingness is one of your most useful tools for life and is indispensable in figuring out what the right path is for you and how to get there. Some people are better than others at hearing and listening to their intuition, but it is possible to hone your intuition. Here are 5 steps to take to hone your intuition.

1. Accept that intuition exists and can help you to reach your goals faster and more smoothly. This is the key. Many people receive intuitive hunches all the time, but they ignore them because they do not believe or do not want to believe that intuition exists.

You have likely had experiences when you've gotten a "gut feeling" or a hunch about someone or something, and later discovered that your hunch was right.

Intuitive Eating

Several years ago I had an instant liking to a man I met on a blind date. I felt a strong feeling for him even before he even spoke. That man is now my husband.

Intuition is very real and listening to your intuition can have big pay-offs. A recent study showed that executives with the highest precognitive ability (intuitive perception) also have the highest profit records.

2. Discover what fears you have that prevent you from using your intuition fully. There are some common fears that come up for people around using their intuition. Some are:

- Maybe you're crazy. You're not. Intuition is a very real thing (see above)

- Maybe you heard wrong. If you create the conditions for you to be able to hear your intuition (see below), this is not likely;

- You can't trust this voice. Sometimes we hear voices in our head that are our intuition feelings and hunches. Sometimes these are voices of fear and ego. Almost always, the intuition is the first voice you hear.

The fear is the one that tries to convince you that the first voice was wrong. If your intuition says "don't trust this person." The other voice will say things like "But so-and-so recommended him" or "But he's accomplished so much. Who am I not to trust him?"

- Other people will think you're crazy. It may feel strange to justify to others the course of action you're taking by simply saying "I have a hunch about this." This will probably seem particularly crazy to other very left-brain dominated people in your life. Do it anyway.

Intuitive Eating

3. Follow your intuition. When you hear that still, small voice or your have inspired thought, act on it. This is really the most important step. If you need to, start practicing with small things -- what should you eat, which movie should you see, etc. After you've tried out your intuitive sense on smaller things, then you can start trusting your intuition to help you with more important decisions and actions. Keep a journal so that you may be able to see patterns that emerge when you have intuitive thought.

4. Take care of your mind, body and spirit. Exercise regularly, eat healthy foods, drink plenty of fresh water, and get adequate rest. The better you take care of yourself, the more receptive you will be to intuitive thoughts. Actually, the more you take care of yourself, the more your brain in general will feel good.

5. Make a practice of having some quiet/meditative time - If you're always rushing about, over-thinking, and overwrought, it's going to be hard for you to hear your intuitive guidance. Make a habit of giving yourself some quiet contemplative time to hear your inner guidance.

WHEN INTUITIVE MEMORIES TAP YOUR CONSCIOUSNESS

Your intuition communicates memories to grab your attention regarding someone or something. Memories are recollections of the past experienced as an observer or a participant. Like a supercomputer, your intuition retrieves remembered, forgotten, and suppressed memories from your soul's archives and delivers them as intuitive messages to help you now.

Whether your memories delight, inspire, sadden, or haunt you, notice when they suddenly pop into your awareness and when you ask the question: "Why am I remembering that?" A significant event occurs in your present life and the past returns with insights. For example, you intuitively see an outer vision show you watching a 1970's movie that dramatizes a remedy for your health issue. Intuitively feel a pulling sensation that indicates a modish business opportunity offers a second chance resembling the one you overlooked six months ago. Intuitively hear your inner voice say, "Accepting that job brings more meaning and bonuses than the hectic position you held in 2006." Intuitively know memories of a previous relationship reveal a new friend's scandalous character. Intuitively taste an aunt's spicy casserole that prepares you for her unexpected and unwelcomed visit. Intuitively smell an earlier vacation's aromas that cause you to laugh away your stress. Intuitively speak, "Letting my dear sister borrow money unnerves me like the bitter night I lost hundreds gambling at a casino." Intuitively sing, "I pay attention while driving and eating so I won't crash into a pine tree like the intoxicated musician I watched on the TV news."

Ancestral memories live in your genetic stream with your own memories. I intuitively dreamed I saw black and white pictures of known and unfamiliar family members; some died before my birth. I never saw those pictures in any relative's photo album but realized they signaled more family history coming to me during my genealogical research.

Some memories belong to others but are accessible through your spiritual connection with everyone and everything. During a dream interpretation class, a friend's husband said, "I have two brothers." I intuitively saw an inner vision show his third brother's face and playfulness-his memory surfaced. I asked him, "Where is your third brother?" He paused and then recalled that another brother had died at a young age.

When intuitive memories tap your consciousness, pay attention to how they apply in your life. Do reminiscences of a beloved high school teacher inspire you to obtain more education? Does a summoned kitchen accident warn you to watch out where you eat dinner? Does a memorized nursery rhyme remind you to be yourself no matter what people say? Even if you experience difficulties recalling certain life events, your intuition knows which memories to retrieve to guide and protect you.

CHAPTER 11

Do Units Acquire Intuition?

This is a fair warning for those not on the spiritual path. Do not read this. A vast majority of scientific thoughts fall into the belief human beings come out of some accidental particles. Then how do particles acquire intuition? It is utterly impossible for inanimate particles to assemble themselves together and create intelligent beings.

Based on reason man is a logical spiritual animal and like animals early in life are generally absorbed in inherent animal cravings. This is why when restless children dig, eat, and move around for no apparent reason in passing their time are animal-like. Some older people behave immaturely like robot zombies who have never grown up emotionally.

Intuitive Eating

People like this can barely communicate with intelligence and are always instinctively acting animal-like instead of with clear and sensible thinking and judgment. Now, some types are like intellectually responsive beings but not uncommon there are some that act more like instinctively motivated animals; when you want to have a conversation with them about money, sex or food they are totally materially minded and reflexively respond like a salivating dog. But when you try to have an important philosophical discussion about the mysteries of God or life their reaction is expressionless as though the conversationalist was stupid.

Watch out for those who have the attracting power of animal magnetism. Some types of snakes use this attracting magnetic power to charm and draw small animals and kill them. All physically minded people are attracted and drawn by animal magnetism. A magnetic exchange of this type between youths of the opposite sex rouses emotions, blinding passions and desires, which produces all types of behavior destructive to them. To allow oneself to mentally or physically fall under the semi-hypnotic influence of someone's animal magnetism is detrimental and one would be constantly blinded by their stronger personality. If the mind is full of prejudice a person can be covertly guided right or wrongly by the judgment of another person.

It is so important never to associate with low life people. Snakes are impervious to their own venom but the poison is deadly to someone who is bitten; the only rational course of action is to exterminate the snakes or never go near them without an antidote. An intelligent man remedies the situation by staying in good company and by separating himself from the companionship of evil animal-like people. We are our own saviors.

Untrained and unguarded ordinary human beings who roam into the terrain of temptations fall imprisoned whether to unexpected aversion and attraction to the senses or likes and dislikes. The science of yoga entreats man to retain a grip of iron on the thought process of his mind where one must not lose self-control even with the utmost provocation.

Development of intuition through concentration hastens human evolution reliably perceiving all truth from within. Real intuition does not require the power of the senses to distinguish truth. With the power of intuition the soul sees directly into all things. All understanding which is obtained through mechanized learning and sense experience from an intellectual viewpoint of man's own power of deduction keeps the truth limited and hard to assimilate. We could spend a lifetime learning through all these modern methods of education which seems like an endless task. Even in a single lifetime no one can learn all the mysteries of heaven and earth with dependence upon the senses and mind, as they do not constantly give an accurate picture. By practicing the methods of concentration with meditation, the faculties of intuition are born where knowing is realized with surprising speed.

Why roam through the endless cycles of incarnations trying to gather intuitional truths entirely depending upon your mind and senses, schools and books to gain knowledge. Learn to awaken your intuition. With the help of the senses of sight and hearing the mind can give false impressions and build mistaken conclusions from its perceptions. The vast ocean cannot be poured into a cup and so the sea of comprehension cannot be emptied into a small cup of intellect. To be able to grasp limitless truth, understanding must be increased by meditation until it progresses into an unlimited cup of perception and intuition.

When a baby grows up the time will come when he has to exercise reason to protect himself. If he misuses his reason an evil outcome is hastened and if guided accurately by good judgment the growing individual becomes happy. Be careful, when your children gain knowledge only through the so-called information superhighway of intellectual smartness their inner pathway to intuition will be blocked and shut off by the hand of self-sufficiency. Education does not consist of letting the young fertile minds full of mush be corrupted by pumping in opinions or thoughts from the contents of books. These young minds are indoctrinated and lied to. Teaching children to develop intuition quickens their own evolution and will help them to recognize truth otherwise they will stay behind powerless to realize their ambitions.

The proof came down from the great scripture writers fully knowing no matter how much study of books they would never be able to directly give ultimate knowledge, but following the path of self-realization and discipline they obtained the wisdom and knowledge by peering through the inner spiritual eye. By learning the intuitive method of study you could assimilate knowledge in a few days that would normally take years.

Take a moment to test yourself, do you know what real and true intuition feels like? Intuition peeps in through the gaps of calmness within your thoughts as an inner voice or haunting feeling as inner whispering. Those developed souls on the path of self-realization know how to distinguish that inner guidance from the delusive imaginary voice of the subconscious mind or human intelligence which endlessly lies to you.

Intuitive Eating

Some people unfortunately depend upon undeveloped or what is called semi-intuition. These people fail to distinguish between a true feeling of intuition and their convictions created of habits like getting the same result as it happened before and intellectual experience. Never be emotional, excited or skeptical as it leads to distortion over clouding intuition. Even men of keen understanding and women of pure feeling typically have semi-intuition. Intuition must be acquired through the path self-realization and meditation.

Who wants to live the animalistic life of unreasoning mundane ordinary people whose life is no better than sleeping, eating and multiplying? With the power of concentration and intuition you can hasten you evolution out of mechanical living, and not by the time honored never-ending process of established academic education. Ignorant children and human adult androids live practically unawakened lives similar to animals. A great way to liberate humanity is for grown-ups who have learned from their own errors to make an effort to rescue children from committing similar mistakes.

There is proof for you and your children to make a distinction when actual truth is told to you. Whenever authentic truth is articulated to you for the first time you absorb as you capture its importance. When told a real truth you think "this sounds like something I have heard before, I think I knew that." Remember all apparently fresh new truths in reality are ancient concealed truths of the spirit and soul and become recognizable again to give us happiness. From the teachings of Paramahansa Yogananda.

CHAPTER 12

Using Your Intuition To Make Decisions To Save Time

If your time is limited and you need to make decisions quickly, try using your intuition. Your intuition can often be right. The hard part is trusting it. Your intuition uses the subconscious mind. But the subconscious mind can see things that your conscious mind can't see. Ever have a hunch about someone or something that didn't make sense logically? But later, it turned out your hunch was correct?

That hunch was your intuition. In fact, many businesspeople use their intuition to make decisions. For example, Donald Trump is a billionaire who makes decisions based on his hunches.

Not only would your decisions be more accurate, but you'll make your decisions faster and save time.

Thinking through a decision and trying to rationalize it is time consuming. If you have a lot of decisions to make, it can take a lot of time to make them. But when you make decisions based on intuition, it only takes a quick flash of "wit." You'll have your decision made in seconds.

As a simple example, let's say you're trying to decide what to eat for dinner. If you think it through rationally, you might start thinking whether you should eat at home or go to a restaurant. Then you'd weigh in the costs and how far away the restaurant is. Then you might think of the quality of the food and the service. After thinking it through, you finally decide to eat at a nearby restaurant.

But let's say you use your intuition instead. You feel in the mood for pizza, and the decision just feels right. So you decide to eat pizza. Within a few seconds, you've already made your decision.

CHAPTER 13

Reasons Why Listening To Your Intuition Is Important!

How many times do you feel like you made the wrong decision? Have you ever had a gut feeling about something but chose not to listen? Or have you ever criticized yourself over and over again because you didn't make the best choice for yourself and feel really bad about yourself?

Not to worry... these experiences are just part of being human and we all experience them! Yet, what is really wonderful about these experiences is that they can be considered a wake-up call for you to find your intuitive path.

It might take a little time to work these experiences out in your life but when you do you will find that your intuition is what drives you to the place of feeling calm, centered and alive. What could be better than that?

And that is not all... you will begin to trust your intuition you stop making the same wrong decisions over and over again, stop over criticize yourself, stop choosing terrible friends that wear you down and stop feeling hopeless, blocked and depressed!

Why is this so important to learn how to find your intuitive path? There are so many reasons and much more than the 7 that I am sharing with you. Just know that an abundant, happy and centered life is available to everyone, including you!

Here are the 7-Reasons Why Finding Your Intuitive Path is Important. Your intuition can help you...

1. Make better decisions!
2. Manage stress, anxiety!
3. Feel more in control!

Intuitive Eating

4. Have a strong sense of self-esteem!
5. Be kind to yourself!
6. Choose your friends more wisely!
7. Choose mindful eating over over-eating!

So here is the thing, rather than having stress, anxiety, self-doubt and more rule your life. Try and change the relationship that you have with your stress! Stop it from being in control of you and learn how to take control of it!

You can then begin to make that shift from fear, stress, suffering and over-abundant mind clutter to a place of peace and full brilliance in your life. You can make these challenges work for you in a positive way.

Now... after knowing why finding your intuition is important you can consciously look at the challenges in your life as teachers instead of crazy roadblocks! Don't wait... take the leap now so that you can reach your full potential, develop your intuition and live a happy and brilliant life!

CHAPTER 14

Ways Your Intuition Talks To You

Your intuition communicates to you every day. Intuition is your natural ability to sense the truth about people, places, things, and situations, without using logic, physical senses, or prior knowledge. While you're awake and asleep, you receive intuitive messages. Whether you're at home or out in the world, you receive intuitive messages. Your intuition talks to you in eight ways:

1) Intuitive seeing is the ability to see visions and dreams showing images that flash like a camera snapshot, pause like a freeze frame, or roll like a motion picture "out in space" or in your mind's eye. For example, you intuitively see a flashing vision show an umbrella or a raincoat to carry with you despite a sunny forecast from local meteorologists.

2) Intuitive feeling is the ability to perceive information via diverse feelings or sensations within your body. This happens with or without you touching external stimuli, a physical agent provoking an interest or a reaction. For example, you intuitively feel a sudden urge to stop in a convenience store to buy a bottle of water. You run into an old friend you haven't seen in years.

3) Intuitive hearing is the ability to hear various sounds "out in space" or in your head (temporal lobes), throat (inner ear), or heart. For example, you ponder a problem while driving to work and intuitively hear a comedic phrase that helps you solve it.

4) Intuitive knowing is the ability to know information without knowing how and without a doubt. Information pops into the top of your head "out of the blue." For example, you intuitively know

an afternoon business meeting will result in an exclusive deal with a new client.

5) Intuitive tasting is the ability to taste various substances without putting anything in your mouth. For example, you intuitively taste sweet honesty or sour dishonesty when questioning your spouse's politics.

6) Intuitive smelling is the ability to smell various scents "out in space" or in your inner nose. For example, you intuitively smell green vegetables to eat for dinner, though you seldom buy them from a farmer's market or grocery store.

7) Intuitive speaking is the ability to speak abrupt, insightful sayings to others and yourself without thinking what to say. For example, you intuitively speak about a natural disaster affecting a country and it happens the next day.

8) Intuitive singing is the ability to sing sudden, edifying songs to others and yourself without hearing external music. For example, you run errands and intuitively sing Arrested Development's song "Tennessee." Then you find out that your next family reunion will be held in Nashville, TN.

When you receive an intuitive message, it's important to be aware of it in progress. Then trust your intuition and act on its guidance. You receive validation instantly or later. The "point of no return" comes when it's too late to act on an intuitive message, no matter the situation. It plays out for better or worse. Your intuition helps you in twenty-eight areas of life, including career, finances, health, and relationships. Stay in the intuitive flow and be blessed.

CHAPTER 15

Eating Disorders - Coaching Yourself To Recovery

Eating disorders, obsession with food, and perfectionism do not always end with a nutrition degree or a 100% raw vegan diet. Yes, removing toxins and processed foods helps-sometimes tremendously-but the pressure to look healthy, thin and beautiful can continue beyond education or dietary shifts. Often, it actually increases.

As a Medical Intuitive and Life Coach, I've encountered many nutritionists and raw fooders who feel ashamed and embarrassed of their ongoing issues with food. As health advocates, they're "not supposed to have these problems anymore!" "Why can't they practice what they preach?" "Why the self-sabotage?"

Secret cooked food binges, bulimia (overeating followed by regurgitation or excessive exercise), dangerously long fasts and detoxification attempts, uncontrollable cravings. This dark side of radiant health can plunge people into a sea of shame and depression-which, of course, they're also not supposed to feel. "What if my clients or readers find out?" they worry.

"You're human," I say. "And it's more common than you think." So common and under-reported, in fact, that I decided to write an article.

Fortunately, our bodies never betray us. They work on behalf of our souls-trying to grab our attention when nothing else has. As with any health concern, once we decode and accept the message, we can let the symptoms go.

Most psychologists recognize these patients' tendency toward perfectionism. Therapy attempts to negate self-judgment. This helps to some degree, but most "recovered" anorexics or bulimics privately confess that the disorder returns whenever they feel out of control. Best case scenario, they can manage the stress and not return to old behavior patterns-but the thoughts remain.

Telling someone to "drop the perfectionism" doesn't provide a cure. In fact, it prevents the cure! Because, truth be told, these people know they can do better. They know they can live bigger, brighter, more influential lives-perhaps more than anyone around them imagines. The quest for perfect body or perfect health reflects a deeper urge to perfect the Self. Successful treatment of eating disorders needs to honor this inner drive-and create a safe space to explore unusual gifts and talents.

Alisson Pot

In a society that feels more comfortable with mediocrity, it often seems easier to transfer the soul's mission to the body. Thus, the anorexic who holds within her a fully compassionate, radiant, healing presence feels less conspicuous as a walking skeleton. The bulimic whose potentially bestselling words of wisdom could transform millions of lives finds it easier to throw up food than to write her book. The personal trainer who intuitively knows how to heal his clients' self-esteem puts all his energy into pumping iron-so that people notice his body rather than his soul. The overweight psychic piles on pounds in order to subdue her too-bright inner glow.

I've noticed a complex yet consistent dynamic in people with eating disorders. Yes, they exhibit perfectionist tendencies, but not in the way most people assume. The shame of imperfection stems less from impaired body image than from living below their natural capabilities. On some level, these people recognize that they have gifts to share, but they get scared. Maybe the world won't accept their unusual talents. Maybe family tells them they need to live a certain way. Perhaps some people find their message offensive. What if everyone thinks they've lost their minds?

Whatever the rational for avoiding their gifts, these perfectionists intuitively know they're not sharing what they could. The shame they express with regard to their bodies or eating habits really mirrors a deeper shame at not living as authentically and compassionately as they could. It doesn't matter if people tell them they look good or consider them experts in their field. It doesn't even matter if they are experts in their field! These people know they could do more, and they feel ashamed for slacking.

Ultimately, it's not really about perfection, though. It's about the "r" word. Responsibility. Having the kind of influence that changes lives can feel scary. Self-sabotage provides both distraction and "proof of unworthiness" to wield such influence. But physical/psychological symptoms can only distract for so long. Eventually, they demand attention, forcing people to deal with those latent gifts. The good news is that people do recover from eating disorders, and you can, too, by augmenting your traditional treatments with targeted personal growth exercises:

1) Practice mindful eating. Pay attention to your food. Notice the flavors, colors, textures and how these make you feel. Ponder all the people and processes involved in the growth and production of your food and express gratitude for the gift on your plate.

2) Start a meditation practice. You can buy a CD like Yogiraj Alan Finger's Life Enhancing Meditations or

Intuitive Eating

Deepak Chopra's SoulofHealing Meditation CD. Both offer excellent guidance in forgiving yourself and others, allowing you to open a bigger, more influential you.

You can also try a kundalini yoga meditation called Sa Ta Na Ma. The words "sa ta na ma" translate roughly to birth, life, death, rebirth, and are thus a powerful transformative mantra. When chanting Sa Ta Na Ma, sit on the floor with your legs crossed and press your elbows to your ribs, so that your arms each form 90 degree angles at your sides. Press the fingertips to the pads on your palms and stick your thumb s up like a hitchhiker. Inhale deeply and then exhale all your air, sucking your navel towards your back. Holding the belly empty, chant silently within yourself four rounds of "Sa Ta Na Ma." Inhale deeply and repeat this process at least six times, up to eleven minutes. The combination of completely emptying and then filling the lungs and belly, combined with the meaning, make this a super technique for people with eating disorders.

3) Whenever you feel "too big" physically, explore your spiritual gifts. If you don't consciously know what these are, ask for guidance. They will reveal themselves! (If you are not Christian, modify the questions for your personal belief system.) People often feel "huge" not because of actual girth but because they have so much unused "stuff" inside of them.

4) When you feel the urge to purge, release in other ways. Honor pent-up energy, words and talents that seek expression. Write, paint, draw, volunteer. Share something beautiful!

5) When you want to starve yourself, "feed" the world. Look at people around you starving for emotional or spiritual nourishment. Offer random

Intuitive Eating

acts of kindness as support. Clean house and donate old clothes. Give until you feel balanced to receive again.

6) If you feel ashamed for your "issues," remember where you're headed. Shame will dissolve as you embrace your deeper purpose and share that beauty with the world. We change the world and our lives one small step at a time. Each day, concentrate on one small step-a journal entry, conversation, or application essay. An outfit of older clothes put together in unexpected ways. A walk in nature. A letter to the editor.

7) If your stomach bothers you, focus on your heart center. If you have trouble getting into your heart, imagine green, gold, or pink light moving in and out of you with your breath. Follow your breath and feel a pulsating warmth in the center of your chest. Let that warmth envelop you and radiate from you like warm, honey, emanating sweetness. Your heart's just

one step above your tummy, but that one step lifts you out of ego and into communion.

CHAPTER 16

Trusting Your Intuition - You Already Know What To Do

There is so much information available to us now that we often get overwhelmed and have trouble making decisions - even small decisions. We have lost the art of trusting our intuition to guide us in making good decisions quickly.

Intuition is a living force which serves as a communication bridge and a language for the deeper, wiser part of you. It provides a truer guidance towards good decisions than our mind can. It uses non-verbal, symbolic methods to communicate. Often we miss this communication - these very subtle promptings - because we are so wrapped up in our thinking mind and our business.

How would you rate your "Intuitive Intelligence" (InQ)? We are all familiar with IQ (Intelligence Quotient) and we hear a lot about EQ (Emotional Intelligence). In contrast to these, your InQ reflects your ability to go inward, respond with a variety of intuitive skills, to perceive connections and subtle realities, and to thrive in the unknown.

While IQ is associated with the brain and EQ with the emotions, InQ is distributed throughout your body. It includes the huge inner territory of your mind, emotions and body. When intuition operates, information flows not from the conscious mind, but from somewhere beyond that mind.

The well known psychologist Carl Jung listed intuiting as one of the four primary ways human beings process reality - in addition to sensing, thinking, and feeling. Intuiting and sensing are methods of direct perception; thought and feeling are somewhat less direct because they involve judgment and evaluation.

For most people, these four functions are not balanced. People tend to have a preference for one function over the other, and also to have one function that is underdeveloped. The majority of people are more easily in the thinking and feeling functions, neglecting their intuitive and sensing functions of perception.

Does this apply to you? Do you spend more time in your thinking, left-brain mind that in your intuitive, creative right-brain mind? If so, that can have implications for your productivity and the effectiveness of the decisions you are making.

The best thinking and decision making is holistic, using both the left and right brain functions. Each hemisphere of our brain has its own area of expertise. The left-brain is expert at verbal, linear, detailed processing. The right-brain excels at non-verbal, spatial, holistic and symbolic processing. You need to gain access to your whole brain - both the left and right hemispheres - in order to actualize your talents, access your fullest potential, and live from an authentic source.

We are all born with intuitive abilities, which can be improved with attention and practice. Your greatest intuitive abilities lie in your body, emotions, visions, silence and joy.

Exploring your intuition involves reconnecting with your internal, natural rhythm and your wise inner self. It means desiring a greater intimacy and connection with the physical world around us that is so full of clues and guidance. As you make time to listen to the soft voice of your intuition, it will welcome you with assistance, creativity and synchronicity.

Intuitive Eating

As you take steps toward making better decisions with the guidance of your intuition, be on the lookout for your logical mind or inner analytical voice wanting to 'put down' or discard the information from your intuition.

Here are some steps you can take to make friends with your intuition, learn its language, and deepen your relationship with your wise inner self.

Let your intuition guide you in making faster, better decisions in your life and in your business. If you feel you've become too 'linear' and think too much before you act, try the following simple exercises to test and strengthen your intuition:

1. If you experience a gut feeling' or a hunch this week, act on it as soon as possible and notice the results.

2. If you are eating out at a restaurant, have the intention that your eyes will fall on the perfect menu choice for you at first glance without having to read the whole menu. Order that item, and notice how satisfying it is.

3. When you are faced with a decision, give your self a 10 minute time limit to make that decision. This will force you to go with your hunch rather than endlessly weighing the pros and cons. Notice how your productivity goes up when you do this.

Complete the following sentences by spontaneously listing things that you already know to do. Rapidly list the first 5 to 10 activities, which come to your mind. Keep them simple and doable, and include both internal and external activities:

"Because my wiser self wants to prepare me for expanded awareness, I already know to . . . . . .

Intuitive Eating

"Because I accept that my wiser self is guiding my intuitive development I already know to . . . . .

"Because I believe my intuition is prompting me, I already know to . . . .

Review your lists, then highlight the one activity from the 1st list which appears most expansive to you, and one each from the 2nd and 3rd lists which attracts you the most right now. Choose a date, time and place to do those activities. Taking action will move your intuition from potential to power.

CHAPTER 17

Relationships: Why Do Some Women Ignore Their Intuition?

It is often said that women are more intuitive than men, and this could be due to a number of reasons. One reason is because they are often more in touch with their feelings. Men on the other hand, are often more logical and out of touch with how they feel.

This is simply a generalisation though; as some men are going to be in touch with how they feel and some women are going to be out of touch with how they feel. And while this much is true, it can still be said that women have a greater connection to their intuition than men do.

Benefits

Having this connection is going to enhance a woman's life in more ways than one. It won't matter what area of their life is in question, as each area of their life can be improved through having it.

So this can be: their career; the relationships they have with others; what they need to eat or avoid and where they should or should not go for example. It will also allow them to know how their loved ones are feeling and if they need anything.

There are many things that intuition can do to improve one's life. Perhaps the main thing it does is allow one to avoid what is not right for them and to experience what it right for them.

Suffering

When one ignores such a powerful source of information, there is the chance that they will suffer in some way. At times this might be minimal, but at other times it could be severe. It can all depend on what it relates to and if there is the chance to do something else once a decision has been made.

Sometimes, it could relate to a decision that is unable to be altered. And at other times, one will still have the opportunity to make another decision.

The Ideal

So the ideal will be for a woman to listen to her intuition, and one area where this will be extremely important is when it comes to their relationships. Through doing this, it will allow her to avoid men who are not right for her or to move on from a relationship that is not healthy.

She may realise that someone is no good for her without needing her intuition. Or it could be a situation where the guy appears to be fine and yet, her intuition is telling her something else. But it won't matter if appearances are deceiving, as her intuition will be there to make sure it doesn't go any further.

Protection

Through listening to their intuition or gut, they are stopping themselves from experiencing a lot of drama and hurt. So their intuition is there to protect them and to keep them out of harm's way.

Problems are going to arise when they completely ignore their intuition. Now, most women are going to have moments where they ignore their intuition, but this is going to be different to when a woman doesn't listen to it at all.

The Wrong Ones

When this happens, a woman is going to have to rely on how men present themselves - appearances will be all important. And while not every man in the world is out to deceive women, not every man has clear intentions either.

This doesn't mean their intuition has therefore completely disappeared; as they could be well aware of it. It is informing them of everything they need to know, but that's as far as it goes. And if they are not listening to their intuition, it means their actions are being defined by something else.

Conflict

If this conflict didn't exist, it would be easier for them to not only listen to their intuition, but to act upon it. And the reason they are experiencing conflict is likely to be due to what is going on for them emotionally.

Emotions can be extremely powerful; so much of what we do as human beings is defined by how we feel. This means that one's intuition can easily be overlooked in favour of ones emotional needs.

Emotional Needs

These emotional needs can be a combination of one's adult needs and the needs that were not met during their childhood. And when it relates to the needs that were not met during their childhood, there is the chance that they will have a lot of power.

So when they meet someone who acts in a certain way, it won't matter if another part of them knows this is nothing more than a facade, as their emotional neediness will take over.

Here, a woman can have the need to be: held, loved, appreciated, validated and accepted, as well as the need to feel safe and secure.

Awareness

Alisson Pot

All the time a woman is emotionally needy, there is going to be the chance that she won't act upon what her intuition is telling her. This means that it will be important for her to process her unmet childhood needs.

As they relate to unmet childhood needs, it will mean that other adults won't be able to meet all of them. They will have to be grieved, as this is done, one will begin to feel less needy.

And this will make it easier for them to work with their intuition, instead of against it. These needs can be grieved with the assistance of a therapist or a healer.

CHAPTER 18

Big Mistakes That Block Your Intuition

Are you aware of your intuition?

One day you are clear as a bell when it comes to trusting your choices and other times it's like staring at a blank wall. I had those days in my past, when I didn't know what was stopping me getting the answers I needed.

Even though I was psychic, I couldn't see what I needed to see because I had blocked my vision. There was I thinking God was punishing me (yes, ridiculous) when in fact the biggest block to clarity was myself.

Are you aware of what blocks your intuition? Everyone has a blind-spot, everyone.

Alisson Pot

The good news is you are not limited by your blocks. It can be effortless to remove blocks that stop you getting what you want now.

Once you've incorporated the 7-steps I give you below into your life and on a consistent basis, you'll no longer feel frustration or dread when it's decision time.

1. Don't Assume Anything

Do you know why you sometimes assume your next best action step?

You THINK you already know the answer.

I often see people settling for the quick-fix. Those people have lack of willingness to discover knowledge and an aura of laziness.

I was one of those people and you know what happened to me?

Intuitive Eating

My goals crashed and burned every time I assumed.

2 Consuming Obsession

Have you ever been into someone, so much so you can't think straight?

In the past, I was always filling my head with a new obsession, usually it was a guy who was no good for me.

I'd think and think and think about what he might be thinking and exhaust myself in the process.

That way, I didn't have to take any RESPONSIBILITY for the decisions I needed to make because I could blame everything on my obsession, truly my distraction.

Can you think of any obsessions you might have that are blocking you from getting the answers you need?

3. Feeling Good About Criticism

Alisson Pot

When you think you know what's best for someone else and they make a mistake, it takes the focus off of your own choices.

Making a comment about how someone eats, speaks, whom they date or what they wear that has a derogatory angle, is being self-righteous.

Criticizing another person is a fast way to disconnect you from higher guidance because when you criticize them, you move your awareness outside of yourself.

Don't tell me you never criticize. Everyone does at times. You'd have to be a saint like Mother Teresa.

Next time you catch yourself criticizing someone with a friend, don't beat yourself up because that's self-criticism. Be aware and stop criticizing.

This will create the space for intuition to exist fully in your life.

4. Being Impatient For The Answer

Do you know what happens energetically when you become impatient?

You disconnect yourself from any wise guidance that is available to you.

One example of impatience is inviting friends over for dinner at 7:00pm and being impatient that it's 6:45pm and they haven't arrived yet.

By the time your guests show up, you're going to be flustered and unreceptive. Now imagine those dinner guests as intuition.

Impatience shuts out your intuition.

5. Swimming In Resistance

Can you see when you enter into your stream of resistance?

You unknowingly push away guidance because when you swim in the stream of intuition, it carries you fast to your answer and goal.

In fact, when you're not used to flowing with intuition, it can feel overwhelming. This is why people choose to stay in resistance.

Any resistance you may be experiencing in your life is only created by you. It is easy to remove with simple techniques that you'll be able to use from the Intuition Development System.

6. A Natural Tendency to Control

Can you see when you are being caring vs. controlling?

It's easy to slip into unknowingly manipulating another person.

In your head you may justify that your intentions are wanting what's best for everyone, however if you're unable to trust another person's ability to make a successful decision, you block your intuition.

When you catch yourself trying to maneuver an outcome, step back and give yourself space for a creative solution.

7. Making Your Fear a Reality

Why fear what you don't know?

Fear manifests itself as an energy you are unaware of or that you don't understand.

Why fear your future?

Fearing what has not been created immerses you in creating the opposite you what you want.

The next time fear arises within you, ask yourself: What's the worst thing that can happen?

I've learned that it's never as bad as you imagine it to be. It only gets very painful when you ignore your fear and go into denial.

Take Responsibility For Your Decisions Now

The more you take responsibility for the decisions you need to make, the greater your intuition will serve you well.

Your first easy step is to OBSERVE how these 7-Big Mistakes may be operating in your life now.

Start using your intuition today to recognize your mistakes and you'll become even more intuitive and confident in the choices you have to make.

CHAPTER 19

Intuitive Leadership - Listening To Your Intuition

Do you ever feel stuck? You are trying to create something new or figure something out but your mind just isn't cooperating. You've got a bad feeling about something but you don't know why. You've got a big presentation coming up and the ideas just aren't flowing. It's like a log jam in there and you can't find a way to set them free. Perhaps if you just keep working at it a little longer, you'll get the answer. Unfortunately, that's probably not going to work.

What you need to do is open your mind to a new set of ideas. When you were little, ideas were endless and you were able to create all sorts of wonderful adventures. You didn't reason your ideas away, you just embraced them. As you got older the powers of reason and rationalization took over. In fact, you now excel at this. You're able to kill any great idea, thought or message you receive within seconds.

The good news is there is a solution. You already have the gift and it's called intuition. It's a natural process that engages the mind. If you can learn to loosen up and trust it, the ideas will come to the surface quite quickly. Everyone is born with it and it connects you to everything else. In fact, it's on call 24-7 and is constantly guiding you. You just need to listen.

To understand how it works, let's take a look at the three components of the brain:

The cerebral cortex (conscious mind) is responsible for your conscious thought, including reasoning, perceiving, imaging and understanding. The limbic system (subconscious mind) is responsible for memory images, mental patterns, fight or flight responses and emotions, such as anger, fear, and pleasure.

The brainstem (unconscious mind) is responsible for basic living functions such as the heart, breathing, eating, and sleeping. The unconscious mind is also the channel of inspiration. When ideas come to us, they find us through the unconscious mind.

When we look at the mind, we observe four processes:

1. Thoughts (conscious)
2. Images (conscious and subconscious)
3. Mental Pattern or Behaviors (subconscious)
4. Emotions (subconscious)

The brain is the functioning physical tool that works within the mind. The brain is a part of the mind. The mind includes inspiration, intuition, sensory instincts and our sixth sense. The mind connects us to collective consciousness and unconsciousness.

So, when we struggle with creation and ideation it's because we're trying to use our conscious mind to resolve it, but it wasn't designed for that task. It's a fabulous problem solver but it's not an ideator. The key to unclogging the log jam is to engage the unconscious mind. The intuition. You can't see intuition because it's energy but it's real and it's always there.

Intuition comes to you as hunch, a gut feeling or a deep knowing. It's like a fleeting whisper. It does not come down with a booming voice like Charlton Heston. You have to be still to hear it. When you operate from a place of intuition you receive ideas and insights that seemingly come out of the blue. That's why ideas come to you when you are driving, taking a shower or walking the dog. When your mind

Intuitive Eating

is focused on another task, your intuition is able to break through and deliver the message.

The thing about intuition is that if you don't listen the first time, it will come back again and again. This is particularly true if something harmful is near. If you get a bad feeling about something or someone then take notice. You're being warned. While it seems like it's your imagination, it's not.

In order to open your receptors to intuitive messages you need to redirect your thoughts. One great method for doing that is to step away from the computer and quiet the mind. Yoga and Meditation are two excellent tools for this. If you're in an office setting you can't exactly get into a lotus position on the floor, but you can stop, move your eyes to a quiet place and take a few relaxing breaths. If possible you can even close your eyes for a minute. Then move away from your frustrating task for a while. Go for a walk, talk to a co-worker or start another task. This will give your brain a chance to relax.

Another strategy is to avoid the same routine every day. Just like muscle memory, you're mind creates its own set of repetitive systems called neural pathways. You want to keep changing things up so that they don't become too well established and stop serving you. Brainstorming, reading new types of books, painting, writing and changing up your physical activity are all great ways to create these new neural pathways while giving space for your intuition to come through.

While all these tools and suggestions are excellent they won't matter if you don't trust the messages you're getting. One way to build trust is to start small. Journal your ideas, hunches and gut feelings and then keep looking back to confirm they were right. This will build your confidence and you'll be more willing to act in the future. You must listen to your intuition. It will tell you everything you need to know.

CHAPTER 20

Core Beliefs That Hinders Overcoming Challenges

There are three main groups of beliefs that hinder a successful approach during challenging times and all these beliefs, if allowed to overwhelm us will breed anxieties and worries, therefore, one has to consciously address them.

The first set of belief is where you see your challenges as menacing. This belief is often displayed where a person beliefs that challenges are a negative occurrences that is not supposed to happen to them, what you will find in such a case, is denial, where one consciously refuses to accept to do something about the situation they are facing but rather gives up.

For some reason, most people tend to approach challenges from a place of worry, and that is an unhelpful approach which negatively affect their opportunities to find the proper solution.

The reasons people respond to challenges from the point of fear, anxiety and worry according to several school of thoughts on the issue of overcoming challenges are attributed to many reasons and excuses. However, to illustrate my points I will use one example that will be familiar to many. For example, being ignorant is one reason why many are struggling to overcome their challenges. That is to say some people are ignorant of the fact that challenges are not unique to them alone but that we all have to face challenges in one degree or form. Of course, there are no doubt that some challenges are just unfortunate circumstances that cannot be explained yet it is no excuse for being in denial or spending the rest of our lives blaming ourselves and others. On the other hand challenges are as a result of our previous decisions. Nevertheless, everyone on earth have to face challenges and so it is a question of how we choose to react to them and the degree of knowledge and skills we have for overcoming them that determines the outcome we get. We all face challenges and this is not unique to anyone in particular, therefore I urge anyone that might be faced with any form of challenges now and are struggling to accept the situation, I want you to know that your particular challenge is not new and others have faced it in the past and many would still face similar challenges in the future therefore I clearly empathise with you and my suggestion would be that you empower yourself through self-reflection and by equipping yourself with knowledge and information that prompts your desired outcome. By refusing to assess and reflect on the situation to find out what options are available, you are simply intensifying the problem and it just won't go away by allowing the circumstances to overwhelm you or by blaming yourself or others.

I will encourage you to stop for a moment and take a good look and think about the environment you are in, then ask yourselves this question. Is there anything around me now that was not created to solve a need? even our breath is a solution to the problem of not been able to live without breathe. In other words, everything around you is a solution to what was once a challenge, which has now been resolved. Wheelchairs was invented because there are people in our society who had challenges walking therefore someone thought of a form of mobility. All the technology and scientific inventions we see today are as a result of overcoming a challenge that existed.

The second hindering belief for overcoming challenges is doubts, some people doubt their ability to solve any problem, as the oldest book the Bible puts it "As a man thinketh, so he is" Therefore, the minute you doubt your ability to overcome your challenges you have blocked your own mind from activating any possible solutions. Also another perspective of looking at this is through the concept of law of attraction. I am a great believer in the law in attraction, I strongly belief being in doubts, denials us of any favourable opportunities been attracted to our path, when you are in constant doubt of your own ability you stop the flow of opportunities and possibilities happening in your direction.. A quote from Sylvia Plath says "And by the way, everything in life is writable about if you have the outgoing guts to do it, and the imagination to improvise. The worst enemy to creativity is self-doubt".

Doubt would deprive you from thinking straight and from identifying the options available to you and above all, the biggest hindrances of all is that it stops you from taking actions. What do they say about inaction, it leads to no action and compounds the problem? A situation you choose not to confront due to doubt will remain the same or worse. To inspire you read this quote that says "Inaction breeds doubts and fear. Action breeds confidence and courage. If you want to conquer fear, do not sit home and think about it. Go out and get busy" By Dale Carnegie

In fact when we are in doubt; fear sets in and deprives from taking any action necessary to overcome the challenges neither does doubt allow us to think creatively for solutions

finally, the third hindrance to overcoming challenges is having negative predictions about the outcome of problem-solving. If you are one of those people who are quick to negatively predict an outcome without even testing it out, you will do so with every strategy, tools, keys, techniques tested and made available to help people overcome challenges. It is not to say every tools, strategies and so on out there works for everyone but we still need to stop doubting and learn to have some element of trust and belief to keep on trying until we find what works for us in overcoming our challenges. However, what hinders people with negative predictions is that they discard every solution so much so that they, themselves would not come up with a solution or problem-solving technique but they will criticise what is available without a proper analysis to back their critiques.

There are several problem-solving questionnaires that would test how one would think and react when confronted with a problem or challenge such as "the negative problem orientation questionnaire by Gosselin, P Ladouceur, R & Pelletier, O. It is important to know that, such questionnaire are not designed to put any one in a box, but for us to review how we might be influenced by our beliefs during challenging times, and knowing how this contribute to the actions we take or how it may stop us from doing something. It is useful to test problem-solving techniques to see whether it can help us to view or do things differently to get a different result.

It safes us time from having to re-invent the wheel when someone else has done the work for us to use and maximise it's potential..

CHAPTER 21

How To Overcome Self-Sabotage And Move Forward

Are you sabotaging yourself out of fear of moving forward? Sometimes although in our conscious minds we think we want to move forward and take action, subconsciously we may be afraid, and as a result this can reflect in all our affairs. For example, a person may find themselves attracting frequent colds, and although they say they want to be well, subconsciously they may be using their colds as an excuse not to go forward and take action with something. They say and even think that they want to move forward on it, but underneath it all, their fear may be holding them back.

You can also sabotage yourself with respect to wealth and success. Even if you've become a good receiver and recognize the sharing aspect of that (i.e. healthy circulation of energy), you may still be afraid of others' reactions to your good fortune, like envy, for example. But the question is, so what if others are jealous of you? If your motives are in the right place and you feel deserving and sharing, others' jealousy is something they need to work through. We cannot downplay our own lives in order to appease those who are displeased about their own circumstances. (It's not about purposely flaunting and bragging about our success with ego motives, but rather freely expressing our passions, creativity and oneness with Source.)

Realize that 1) you deserve your success as it is a natural state of being, 2) you cannot please everyone. Everyone must take responsibility for their own lives and blaming you for their troubles or being jealous of your success is not going to be the path to their success, 3) it is not your job to lower your vibration to match and please those in that lower state of consciousness (i.e. lack). Your moving down the ladder to meet a lower state of consciousness will not help the person in need, but it can result in your own depreciation of energy.

Another fear for some is that they will not be liked if they become successful; they fear losing their friends for example. But if someone is truly your friend, it needn't matter how much money, success or fame you have, right? A true friend would be happy for you. Look, we are all here to be fulfilled. We are all here to be co-creators. We are all here to share our gifts with the world. We are not here to feed into ego demands and lack mentality. We are not here to please everyone by compromising or sabotaging ourselves. So don't worry about the approval of others or trying to please everyone. Just be true to yourself and shine from there.

Another self-sabotaging emotion involves feeling guilty for having, while some others have less. Some people get very passionate about saving the world (which is a noble plight), and they feel the way to do this is to deprive themselves of sustenance (not so noble). This can turn into very ego-centric and self-righteous behavior. To think that by depriving yourself or by condemning money you will somehow save the world is truly backwards thinking. All you truly end up doing is adding one more person to the problem, i.e. you. It would be like purposely keeping yourself poor in order to make a statement about poverty. Do you really think that the poor person wants you to be poor too? What will you have to give those in need if you purposely sabotage yourself?

Instead, be a solution-oriented person. Know that the more you have the more you have to share. Think of it as respecting and honoring yourself, and being able to care for others as a result. It's about feeding yourself and then sharing your 'food' and energy with others. You can help others better if you are in a position to actually help. Look at the contributions of Oprah, Bill Gates, and Warren Buffet. All these people have it to give it, and so they do. It's not about depriving yourself of money, but rather choosing what you do with it.

The solution is this:

1) feel deserving,

2) realize you are not depriving anyone of having by having (as long as you act with integrity of course),

3) know you have made the choice to align with source and feed your consciousness with pleasant thoughts, and that everyone has that same choice. The fact that you are attracting like experiences to that choice is law, if others choose differently, it is not something for which to feel guilty. What you have is meant for you since you have it,

4) know that the more you have, the more you have to share. Dragging yourself down to match a lower vibration does not serve anyone.

The truly sharing thing to do is to be successful. Know that enjoying your life and all your G-d-given blessings is G-d's will for you and you are honoring your true self and G-d by doing so. Feeding into others' insecurities and misguided feelings does not help them or you. The best thing you can do is to be proactively grateful for all that you have, share to the best of your knowledge and ability, and wish all those people who are yet to discover laws of mind and nature a smooth path of transformation and joy. Thinking that depriving yourself or keeping yourself down will help others is backwards thinking. You actually do them a greater service by being happy and successful.

Alisson Pot

Know that G-d is your source, and that G-d is everyone's Source too. It's not an elite club. We all have access.

Others' lack has nothing to do with you or what you have. You may be the catalyst to awaken desire and transformation in others. Your job is to be yourself and live your life with integrity and joy. Be loving, non-judgmental and forgiving, wishing others well. Fulfill your destiny and help others along the way. Feel free to enjoy your joy and all your wonderful blessings and good fortune, after all, it is G-d's will for you and you should be proud of yourself for allowing it in.

Everyone chooses their circumstances from a spiritual perspective and everyone has access to, and is already one with Source and all goodness. It simply boils down to awareness, and if you have it and are doing something with it, you have every right to enjoy it. And through your enjoyment and happiness you also share with the world.

Sure maybe some people's circumstances lend an easier time to re-learning the universal principles, but if you are that person who receives this knowledge and benefits from it, then you are in an advantageous position to share your knowledge with others. If you purposely put yourself in the same place vibrationally as those who are not yet enlightened, you are hurting them and you are hurting yourself. It just doesn't make sense to do things that way.

Bottom line, we can do/be/have anything we desire in life and the only limits placed on us are the ones we impose on ourselves.

CHAPTER 22

Understanding, Developing And Using Our Intuition

How to Develop your INTUITION is a beginner's course.

Let's begin with being able to understand exactly what INTUITION is.

Let's Define INTUITION

Is this a magical facility? Some mystical power?

Is it an angel that sits on our shoulder taking care of us?

R. Buckminster Fuller the late philosopher and creator of the geodesic dome, called intuition "cosmic fishing." He went on to explain that once you feel the nibble you have to hook that fish.

Intuitive Eating

Allot of people he said just get a hunch and then light a cigarette, and forget about it.

Zen Buddhist describe it as;

"the sound of one hand clapping"

Police detectives describe it as " a gut feeling"

The words are different but the underlying meaning is the same.

Intuition is knowledge, that is gained without rational thought, you know the example I just feel it, or I know it, or I have that feeling .... since it comes from some level of awareness just below our conscious level it is really hard to define it is elusive and always just out of reach...

Intuition comes from a place that is not known to us yet, if we were put under hypnosis we could recall things that we did not even know we were gathering. We really do know things we do not know...

We gather all these impressions, they cannot be verbalized or even understood, but they guide our actions.

Even if we cannot really put into words, what we are feeling, and although it may be foggy and in our subconscious mind, our impressions come from a deep, deep place in our mind, they do not manifest by accident.

It was pulled from neither a big empty place nor a void; it was with in us, deep and natural....

We have years of ideas, facts, our relationships, what we encountered, along this path of our life... our mind organizes it and keeps track of it.

Intuitive Eating

Along this path that is not charted, intuition literally compresses all this learning all this experience we have and gives it to us in an instantaneous flash OF what we call INSIGHT, our deepest mind calling out to our highest intellect.

There are those people who order their subconscious mind to do what they want, to come up with solutions, with answers, and they get them. Have you ever done that?

In addition, others still have self-fulfilling wishes such as when I eat this it will go to my hips. Surely, we all know this one, right.

Our minds are vast, and deep, secret, and yet so simple, if we can just begin to understand. It is all within us.

In the business world, most CEO's know that it takes more than just logic to run a business; it takes

Alisson Pot

INTUITION and also trust in your self, to believe that some part of you knows.

Edgar Mitchell astronaut, is a very strong believer in Intuition, having come back from space, being the sixth astronaut on the moon. Mitchell knows that Man's potential knowledge is allot more than the five senses. It is INTUITION coupled with everything else.

Mitchell was using both kinds of vision, inner and outer, the physical and the minds eye, as he gazed upon the earth from the moon he saw that earth's ills would only be curable by INTUITION. That is a huge statement, for him to announce.

Hopeless if he just sticks to his analytical approach.

He still speaks highly and most feverishly of this mysterious and most creative process, which works outside, mans conscious awareness, of which he is most assured will fix all of our problems.

Which is INTUITION.

Intuition is that and a whole lot more... it is that gut feeling that inner knowing when you should be or should not be doing something. Mitchell went on to say that when they the astronauts were studying plans for the missions they spent ten percent of there time in a logical manner, and ninety percent of their time learning how to react intuitively to all the what if's.

However, he went on to claim that reliance on the intuition and intuitive response was the most important part of the training for the astronauts.

Recognizing that there is the existence of INTUITION is a positive and big first step next is having faith in the fact that answers to even the toughest of problems will leap completely conceived into our awareness, and always when you least expect it.

INTUITION is our sixth sense some say. I would like to say that it is our first sense.

How you may ask, or why, well when we are in the womb, in the dark in the stillness we are forming, into whom we will be, "we know," what will follow when we are released from this place of warmth and comfort, and what is to follow.

We KNOW. The cold and bright lights, the sterile conditions that allot of us face as we enter this world, the birthing rooms, and the world at large.

We KNOW when we are in the womb, what is out there...

WE KNOW.

Intuitive Eating

Yet when we are in the womb, we know. There are those who remember. INTUITION as the -first sense- makes more sense to me, before we can smell, speak, hear, touch, and taste before all that

we KNOW... we KNOW..............we KNOW....

Exercise:

Write down in a notebook all your feelings of things that you KNOW for example...

You KNOW who is calling you on the phone.

You KNOW who is at your door before you answer it.

You KNOW where your kids really are, :) if they tell you they were someplace else.

You KNOW when someone is coming to visit you before they drive up the driveway.

Alisson Pot

You KNOW what your spouse is making for dinner.

You KNOW what, who, when, where

Most of us really do not have any idea just HOW MUCH WE DO KNOW until we begin write it down.

When you begin to document it, you begin to understand what role INTUITION Plays in your life..

Webster's Dictionary Describes Intuition as:

INTUITION IS looking upon, seeing with the physical eyes. The eye of the mind, contemplation, sight, an indirect view, regard, reference.

INTUITION IS knowledge obtained, or the power of knowing, without recourse to reference or reasoning, it is innate or instinctive knowledge, insight, familiarly, either quick or ready, or it is apprehension.

Intuitive Eating

INTUITION IS immediate apprehension, or cognition, either the faculty or power of such apprehension or a particular act or instance of it.

INTUITION IS applied to direct or immediate knowing, whether mystical, perceptional, intellectual, or moral, and is in general, contrasted with speculative, reflective.

CHAPTER 23

Sleep Deprivation - The Facts

How many hours do you think you are supposed to be sleeping each night? What do you think you are supposed to eat or drink before you go to bed? What about television, music, books, and other types of entertainment in the bedroom? You have likely had the stereotypical answers to all of these questions drilled into your head over the years, but the real facts about sleep deprivation may surprise you.

Let's start with how many hours of sleep you should be getting each night. If you think you are sleep deprived because you are not getting the standard 8 hours a night, stop beating yourself up. Not everyone needs 8 hours of sleep!

What matters more than the number of hours you spend in bed is the quality of those sleeping hours. You could sleep for 10 hours and wake up feeling exhausted, or sleep 6 and wake up ready to tackle the day. Forget about the number of hours and focus on getting a higher quality sleep and you are more likely to overcome sleep deprivation.

As for what you should be eating or drinking before bed, it once again comes down to your individual body. The common advice is to never eat a heavy meal close to bedtime, but if having a full stomach gets you drowsy ignore the stereotype and do what works for you.

Finally, it is a good idea to take distractions out of the bedroom so your sleeping hours are deeper and more restoring. That said, if you are relaxed and soothed into sleep with calming music, then play it quietly. If you enjoy reading a chapter or two to unwind, go for it. Just make sure the light switch is close at hand so you don't have to get up and walk across the room before tucking under the covers.

Sleep deprivation is a very personal matter, so do what works for you!

REFERENCES

DeVillera, Julia. GirlWise. Roseville, California: Prima Publishing; 2002.

Gaesser, Glenn. Big Fat Lies: The Truth about Your Weight and Your Health. New York: Ballantine; 1996.

Hersh. Sharon A. "Mom, I feel fat!" Colorado Springs, Colorado: WaterBrook Press; 2001.

Hutchinson, Marcia. 200 Ways to Love the Body You Have. CA: Crossing Press; 1999.

Jacobs-Brumberg, Joan. The Body Project: An Intimate History of American Girls. NewYork: Random House; 1997.

Jantz, Gregory L. Hope, Help & Healing for Eating Disorders. Colorado Springs, Colorado: Waterbrook Press; 2002.

Omichinski, Linda. Staying off the Diet Roller Coaster: Advicezone.com; 2000.

Rhodes, Constance. Life Inside the Thin Cage. Colorado Springs. Colorado: Waterbrook Press; 2003.

Quart, Alissa. Branded: The Buying and Selling of Teenagers. Cambridge, Massachusetts: Perseus Books Group; 2003.

Tribole, Evelyn. Intuitive Eating: A Recovery Book for the Chronic Dieter. New York: St. Martin's Press; 1995.

WEBSITES AND PROGRAMS

Do not go yet; One last thing to do

If you enjoyed this book or found it useful I'd be very grateful if you'd post a short review on it. Your support really does make a difference and I read all the reviews personally so I can get your feedback and make this book even better.

Thanks again for your support!

Made in the USA
Lexington, KY
31 August 2019